Understanding American Political Parties

How do parties respond to the electorate and craft winning strategies? In the abstract parties are the vehicles to make democracy work, but it is often difficult to see the process working as well as we think it might. Indeed, voters often struggle to see parties as the valuable vehicles of representation that so many academics describe. There is a clear discrepancy between the ideal expressed in many textbooks and the reality that we see playing out in politics.

Noted scholar Jeffrey Stonecash gives us a big picture analysis that helps us understand what is happening in contemporary party politics. He explains that parties behave the way they do because of existing political conditions and how parties adapt to those conditions as they prepare for the next election. Parties are unsure whether realignment has stabilized and just what issues brought them their current base. Does a majority support their positions and how are they to react to ongoing social change? Is the electorate paying attention, and can parties get a clear message to those voters? This book focuses on the challenges parties face in preparing for future elections while seeking to cope with current conditions. This coping leads to indecisiveness of positioning, simplification of issues, repetition of messages, and efforts to disparage the reputation of the opposing party. Stonecash sheds much needed light on why parties engage in the practices that frustrate so many Americans.

Jeffrey M. Stonecash is Maxwell Professor of Political Science at Syracuse University. His research focuses on political parties, realignment of their electoral bases, and the impact of changing alignments on the nature of policy debates.

Understanding American Political Parties

Democratic Ideals, Political Uncertainty and Strategic Positioning

Jeffrey M. Stonecash
Maxwell School, Syracuse University

 Routledge
Taylor & Francis Group

NEW YORK AND LONDON

First published 2013
by Routledge
711 Third Avenue, New York, NY 10017

Simultaneously published in the UK
by Routledge
2 Park Square, Milton Park, Abingdon, Oxon OX14 4RN

Routledge is an imprint of the Taylor & Francis Group, an informa business

Library of Congress Cataloging in Publication Data
Stonecash, Jeffrey M.
   Understanding American political parties: democratic ideals,
   political uncertainty and strategic positioning/Jeffrey M. Stonecash.
   p. cm.
   Includes bibliographical references.
   1. Political parties–United States. I. Title.
   JK2265.S75 2012
   324.273–dc23
   2012012711

ISBN: 978-0-415-50844-5 (hbk)
ISBN: 978-0-415-50843-8 (pbk)
ISBN: 978-0-203-12344-7 (ebk)

Typeset in Bembo
by Florence Production, Stoodleigh, Devon

Printed and bound in the United States of America by
Walsworth Publishing Company, Marceline, MO.

Contents

Preface

We have an ideal about the role political parties should play in American democracy. They are expected to present alternatives and organize and lead policy debates. The electorate then reacts and renders its judgment, providing feedback to elected party members as they move to considering policy choices. While that ideal is regularly presented in textbooks, much of the American public has serious doubts about how well parties fulfill this ideal. They see simplistic proposals, negative ads, squabbling, and confrontations in Congress that do not seem to focus on and resolve problems. The reality does not appear to meet the ideal. The concern of this book is why does that seeming discrepancy exist? Why do parties engage in behaviors we don't like?

The answer involves the political conditions that parties face as they approach upcoming elections and seek a majority. These conditions and the resulting uncertainty create behaviors many do not like. We have many excellent studies that interpret what has happened in the past and how we got to where we are. They track the concerns and policy positions of the parties over time and how electoral groups change their partisan support in response. As valuable as those studies are, they miss something essential to understanding how American political parties see the political world and act. Studies invariably look backward, trying to interpret why some trends have happened.

Party politicians also look back to try to understand how they got to where they are, but they are enormously preoccupied with assessing existing conditions and deciding what positions they should take as the next election approaches. They must decide what issues and positions might help them connect with enough voters to achieve a majority. They draw upon the past, but they have to focus on what will work for the future.

The conditions they face are: awareness that considerable change has occurred over time in who is voting for each party; uncertainty whether this change is over; diverse interpretations of what brought them the base they have; an ongoing lack of a majority; continuing social change that they are uncertain how to react to; a disengaged electorate; and, a fragmented media that may not convey the positions the parties stake out. These conditions prompt strategies and behaviors that much of the electorate does not like, but that parties see as a necessary part of coping with the conditions they face.

The following chapters review the conditions just listed and the behaviors that each prompts. The focus is on what party leaders and members face and how they are likely to see the political context within which they operate. It is an uncertain world and parties operate with much more of a trial and error approach than many of the historical interpretative analyses sometimes suggest. If this book has virtues, they are approaching the political world from the perspective of party leaders thinking about future elections and explaining why they behave the way they do.

Ultimately the important question is whether, despite these behaviors, the parties play out the ideal roles in democracy that we expect. That will be taken up at the end.

Part I

American Political Parties

Democratic Ideals and Doubts

The rise of political parties is indubitably one of the principal distinguishing marks of modern government. The parties . . . have been the makers of democratic government. . . . political parties created democracy and modern democracy is unthinkable save in terms of the parties.[1]

If I could not go to heaven but with a party, I would not go there at all—Thomas Jefferson.

The two parties can't come to a consensus even when the solution is obvious.[2]

A majority of Americans say it's more important that political leaders in Washington compromise in order to get things done, rather than stick to their beliefs, even as Congress heads for a government shutdown for the second time in less than two months because of partisan disagreements.[3]

1 Democracy and the Ideal Role of Political Parties

The fundamental premise of democracy is that the opinions and interests of people matter. At one time emperors, kings and religious authorities were presumed to possess wisdom and to be more capable than their subjects. Elites were seen as best suited to govern and the masses should defer to them. Democracy grew as a direct challenge to this idea that elites had a monopoly on wisdom. Elites were challenged as having no inherent right to determine what policies government should enact. Individuals had legitimate and differing views and their opinions should matter when decisions were made. Rather than the people listening to and accepting the decisions of elites, the rise of democracy meant that elites are expected to listen to and treat as legitimate the views of the people.[4]

The simple proposition that people's views matter, however, did not answer the question of how their views were to be communicated. We have a representative democracy and not a direct democracy. We elect and largely rely upon politicians who seek to interpret what people want, so politicians must find a way to discern public views. We could rely on mass gatherings but how can someone interpret what opinions exist in that gathering? We could rely on letter writing by constituents but who knows the opinions of those who do not write? We could elect people as individuals and try to sort out all the views of those elected, but with so many elected in America, the sorting through all these separate voices to discern what voters meant would be a challenge. The means of conveying public opinions is a fundamental challenge within democracy.

The situation is further complicated in that there are significant disagreements about what policies should be adopted. The challenge is not just to find out what "the people" want but to find a way to sort through differing views of what policies should prevail and find a way to represent them. Some believe that the federal government should play an active role in responding to social problems, while others believe that society works best if government is restrained, the national government in particular is limited, and individuals are encouraged to solve their own problems. Those who hold these opposing views do not hold them casually. They believe that the future of a free and democratic society hinges on whether their views are followed in setting policies for the society. Others hold no clear opinions on these issues, making a debate more complicated.

It is the presence of differing and strongly held views about what society should do that prompted political parties as a solution.[5] If a group believes in their views they want their views represented because they think these policies are better for the nation. They may see a neglected social problem and think that a policy should be adopted to address it. Pollution levels are seen as too dangerous and policies are necessary to limit the ability of companies to pollute. Those who are younger or with lower incomes lack health insurance. A group may seek new government policies to respond to these perceived problems. Or a group may seek to mobilize to oppose and critique existing policies. Taxes and regulations are too high and are seen as stifling entrepreneurs. Opponents believe someone needs to call attention to the negative effects of this on society. They believe it will be beneficial to everyone to have someone present a critique of the policies in existence. The challenge in a democracy is to find others with similar views and demonstrate broad support for their position.

If they can band together and create a common identity party members can also work toward solving the problem of mobilizing support. It is not enough to just make an argument about the need to do something. The need is to find those who agree with these positions and demonstrate that there is widespread support for these views. They believe in something and see the issue as an opportunity to create support that might endure. A Democrat believes that workers should get a minimal wage rate and wants to enact a minimum wage. If they can make this a campaign focus it may garner some attention among some who might support the idea but have not seen politics as relevant and create political support. In the 1936 presidential election President Franklin Roosevelt and his Democratic Party campaigned on a minimum wage, which was eventually enacted in 1938. It created more support for President Franklin Roosevelt and made the conditions of workers part of public discussions. Republicans wanted this to remain a matter for employers and employees to work out without the mandates of a national law. This process of Democrats seeking to represent workers expanded the scope of what was considered a public matter.[6] It also brought Roosevelt continuing support from urban workers.[7]

In the 1980s, following the Supreme Court decision *Roe v. Wade* in 1973, which made abortion legal and a private decision, many conservatives thought that allowing this practice was immoral. They saw it as a matter that should not just be left to individuals but as one for which there should be a public social policy. They wanted to bring it back to the public arena and have Congress enact legislation making it illegal. Some Republican candidates agreed with them and saw this as a chance to increase their support among social conservatives. They gradually increased their comments about the importance of limiting or banning abortion and their support among social conservatives increased.[8] An issue once banned and then allowed by the court decision was brought back to the public arena by those troubled by a decision making it legal. In advocating for limiting abortion, Republicans were seeking to attract opponents of abortion who had not previously voted Republican. The process of a party seeking support for a position brought about representation of an issue and those concerned about it. The result was more of a debate about whether abortion should be allowed.[9]

If a party can create some internal consensus on an issue they can in turn present that position to voters. This may involve considerable simplification—abortion is immoral or a woman's decision, government intrusion is beneficial or detrimental to society—but it allows the presentation of a general principle to voters. This makes it possible to present voters with a simple message that conveys broad principles, which makes it easier for voters to connect with either party. Some voters will be reluctant to accept these two simplistic alternatives, but for the bulk of voters these alternatives may well constitute meaningful choices. The formation of a clear party position solves a communication problem.

If the party creates a clear identity it will allow them to mobilize sympathetic voters. It may get them interested enough to identify with the party, contribute to it, perhaps work for the party, and to turn out and vote for the party. To achieve these goals, the party must make sure it is focusing on concerns important to a substantial segment of the electorate. If a party focuses on matters that are not important to voters it is unlikely to prompt their support and garner their votes. The need for votes should function to keep a party focused on issues relevant to voters.

The Dynamic

If this process works as we hope, the following dynamic occurs. Party leaders hold certain beliefs about what government policy should be. These leaders interact with and listen to activists. They may conduct polls to verify whether a substantial segment of voters agree with positions they support. If they find this support, the party members discuss among themselves whether to make this a theme during the upcoming campaign. Those who are running for various offices consider how much they agree with a theme and how much they wish to be identified with the theme. Perhaps each party is comprised of those who generally share the same views about the proper role of government. Most candidates then decide to campaign on the same general theme.

Throughout a campaign each party's candidates present their views of the role of government. The voters then render their judgment of which party they support or do not support. Out of this process comes a majority party that then assumes power over government. If during the campaign candidates of the party winning a majority express roughly the same policy positions,[10] the presumption is that there is support for their proposals.

The party can assume they have support from the electorate for their positions.

If this works as indicated, and a party wins the presidency, the Senate, and the House, it can contribute to overcoming one of the central problems of American democracy: separation of powers within the national government. When American institutions were formed, one of the central concerns was that American colonists had experienced national governments that were too powerful, that could intrude in people's lives too much. Government was seen as an institution that deprived people of freedom. The solution was to create separate institutions, each with some ability to check the power of the others.[11] To the extent that power was dispersed it would be harder to pass legislation and intrude on personal freedoms. This separation of powers can work very well, and over time many have worried about the inability of American government to respond to problems because one party will control Congress and another the presidency, creating a stalemate.[12] If elected officials come from the same party and share the same views then they can propose and enact legislation that reflects their positions. The argument is that the party label gives voters the chance to put like-minded voters in power so something can be accomplished in response to problems.

The majority party then prepares for and conducts the next campaign with a focus on having fulfilled their policy promises. The opposing party, perhaps still believing that the majority of voters do not really support what has been done, presents critiques of what has been done. The minority party may present what they see as the flaws in the policies adopted. The voters then render their judgment, and the cycle begins again.

The result should be a process in which party leaders and candidates, with their own beliefs, interact with activists, interest groups, and voters to assess just what views exist in the public. Candidates must be attentive to what the public thinks because they need votes. They must assess whether a majority supports their views, whether they need to adjust their positions, or whether they need to be careful in how they present their views. Campaigns are the vehicles for presenting ideas and positions to voters. Voters in turn render their reaction. A majority is chosen, presumably reflecting what the majority of voters want. This presentation becomes a justification for taking action if a party wins a majority.

The central premise of democracy, that voters matter, is fulfilled. A party must secure a majority vote from the electorate before it can acquire power to change policies. Parties may err sometimes in their judgments but in the long run this process should keep policies roughly in accord with majority views in the society.

Some Examples

1930–1932: This ideal of how the process might work has actually played out numerous times in American history. In October 1929 a major economic

Table 1.1 Republican Fortunes, 1928–1932

	Year of Elections		
	1928	*1930*	*1932*
House			
Seats won	270	218	117
% of seats	62.1	50.1	26.9
Senate			
Seats won	56	48	36
% of seats	58.3	50.0	37.5

American collapse began. Republicans had dominated American politics for most of the prior 30 years. Republican Herbert Hoover was president, elected in 1928. Both houses of Congress were held by Republicans. The dominant economic thought of the time was that markets adjusted by themselves if left alone. This was very compatible with conservative Republican thought; that individuals should be encouraged to adjust and take care of their own problems. President Hoover adhered to the belief in the ability of private markets to adjust, as did the remainder of his party. As economic decline persisted, the Republican Party continued to affirm their faith in private markets and offered no programs to respond.[13] As the party in power, the electorate assessed their position in the 1930 and 1932 elections and the judgment was not positive (Table 1.1). A party stood for a policy and was soundly rejected. From 1928 to 1932 their percentage of seats in the House declined from 62.1 to 26.9 and from 58.3 to 37.5 in the Senate. It was clear what the electorate thought of the Republican position. The public chose the symbol of the Democratic Party label as a better alternative than the Republicans.

1964: In 1964 the Republican Party presented Barry Goldwater as their presidential candidate. He reflected a growing conservative movement within the Republican Party. Conservatives felt the party was too accommodating to Democrats. Goldwater clearly stood for less government and specifically opposed the 1964 Civil Rights bill, which addressed problems of inequality of rights for blacks. The party was by no means united in its support for Goldwater, but the party had been struggling to escape minority status since the 1930s and many felt it was time to present a clear alternative.[14] President Lyndon Johnson presented a clear alternative by supporting the Civil Rights bill and many other liberal programs. Goldwater's image and his positions were dominant in the election, and Republicans lost the presidential contest and experienced a decline in their percentage of House and Senate seats (Table 1.2). The conclusion of Democrats was that they had a mandate to do what President Johnson had presented.[15]

1992–1994: In 1992 Democrat Bill Clinton was elected president and chose to make expanding access to health care a major initiative. Democrats

Table 1.2 Republican Fortunes, 1960–1964

	Year of Elections		
	1960	*1962*	*1964*
House			
Seats won	174	176	140
% of seats	40.0	40.5	32.2
Senate			
Seats won	36	34	32
% of seats	36.0	34.0	32.0

controlled both houses of Congress. He appointed a task force in 1993 that began creating new regulations and legislation to achieve his goal. As the process unfolded, Republicans, conservatives, and interest groups criticized the effort as inappropriately expanding the role of government and giving government officials too much control over individual medical issues. While Bill Clinton emphasized fairness and providing health care to those who lacked it, opponents stressed their fears about government intrusion and the loss of individual freedom. As the process continued, Democrats in Congress, despite their general sympathy with the goal, became nervous about being seen as favoring "big government" and the legislation was never enacted. The years 1993 and 1994, however, were dominated by arguments about the legislation, with the parties taking opposing sides. Each party presented a relatively clear image of where they stood on the issue.[16]

The 1994 elections were seen by many as a verdict on the Clinton effort. Democrats had 57 of 100 Senate seats in 1994 and after the election they lost the majority and held 48 seats. Democrats had held a majority in the House since 1954. Republicans took the majority in the 1994 elections, increasing their seats from 176 of 435 (40.5 percent) to 230 (52.9 percent). There are always disputes about the meaning of elections, but the reaction of voters to the health care issue was important. In 1992 and 1994 voters were presented with this survey question:

> There is much concern about the rapid rise in medical and hospital costs. Some people feel there should be a government insurance plan, which would cover all medical and hospital expenses. Suppose these people are at one end of a scale, at point 1. (Others feel that medical expenses should be paid by individuals and through private insurance plans like Blue Cross or some other company paid plans). Suppose these people are at the other end, at point 7. Of course, some people have opinions somewhere in between at points 2,3,4,5 or 6. Where would you place yourself on this scale, or haven't you thought much about this?

Table 1.3 Responses to Health Care Question and Voting in House Elections, 1992 and 1994

Position	Distribution of Q Responses			Percent Voting Democratic		
	1992	*1994*	*Change*	*1992*	*1994*	*Change*
1 (govt)	17.8	12.0	−5.8	72.8	74.1	1.3
2	13.6	7.8	−5.8	73.1	61.6	−11.5
3	13.9	10.1	−3.8	67.4	62.8	−4.6
4	18.1	20.5	2.4	53.6	49.2	−4.4
5	10.8	14.2	3.4	42.9	39.1	−3.8
6	8.9	14.4	5.5	41.3	30.6	−10.7
7 (individ)	7.2	16.2	9.0	40.8	21.9	−18.9
1–3	45.3	29.9	−15.4	71.2	67.0	−4.2
5–7	26.8	44.8	18.0	41.8	30.1	−11.7

Source: ANES 1948–2008 Cumulative File.

The responses and how those people voted in the 1992 and 1994 House elections are presented in Table 1.3. The table first presents the percentage choosing the responses of 1 (strong support for government role) through 7 (individual responsibility) for 1992 and 1994. The right side of the table indicates how individuals with different opinions about this issue voted in 1992 and 1994 for Democratic House candidates. Two changes occurred between 1992 and 1994 that conveyed voters' reactions to politicians. The emergence of the issue of who should provide health care and the criticisms of Republicans and interest groups had an effect on public opinion. The distribution of opinion shifted away from the Democratic view that government should play a role and toward the view that individuals should be responsible. In 1992, 45.3 percent of voters chose positions 1–3 (more favorable to government) and 29.9 percent chose positions 5–7 (more favorable to individual responsibility). The rest had no opinion. In 1994 the respective percentages were 29.9 favorable to a government role and 44.8 favorable to an individual role. The percentage more favorable to individual responsibility increased by 15 points over two years. Republicans took a stance against government involvement and were able to significantly shift public opinion. Parties can play a role in making an argument about an issue and shaping, to some extent, public opinion.

As the Republican Party presented itself as opposed to more government involvement in health care, this clarity brought them a greater percentage of votes among those who were more inclined to see individuals as responsible for securing health care insurance. Among those choosing 5–7 on the scale, 58.2 percent voted Republican in 1992. In 1994, with greater clarity of their position, Republicans secured the votes of 69.9 percent of this group. Republicans staked out a position against a policy proposal and benefited in two ways. They increased the percentage agreeing with their

Table 1.4 Opinions on the Iraq War and George Bush and Republican Fortunes in
2006

Vote in 2006 House Elections

	Democrat	*Republican*
War in Iraq opinion		
Approve	18	81
Disapprove	80	18
George Bush job approval		
Approve	14	84
Disapprove	82	16

position and secured a higher percentage of votes among those agreeing
with their position. Republicans took the campaign and the election results
as an indication there was more support for conservative positions.[17]
President Bill Clinton appeared to accept that conclusion and in his 1996
State of the Union address he declared that "The era of big government is
over."

2006: Following the 9/11 attacks on America, the Bush administration
decided in 2003 to attack Iraq, arguing that Saddam Hussein and Iraq were
a threat to America and might possess weapons of mass destruction.
Democrats, following the fear created by the 9/11 attacks, were reluctant
to be seen as strong opponents of the attack. While initially the March 2003
attack on Iraq was seen as successful, no weapons of mass destruction were
found and a relentless internal war by insurgents within Iraq made it difficult
for the administration to claim things were going well. Gradually, Democrats increased their criticism of the war effort in Iraq. The 2006 elections
became in many ways a referendum on the war and the administration's
handling of subsequent events in Iraq.[18] President George Bush and congressional Republicans had staked their reputations on the war.

Opinions about the Iraq War and George Bush were strongly associated
and they had a powerful role in voting decisions. By November 2006, 40.4
percent approved of the war and 59.7 percent disapproved. George Bush's
job approval ratings were at 38 percent. Those who approved of the war
and of George Bush voted very strongly for Republican House candidates.
Those who disapproved of both voted very strongly for Democratic House
candidates. The parties in Congress were diverging in their opinions about
the war and President Bush and voters used party labels to register their
reactions. Given the majorities disapproving of what George Bush and
Republicans were doing, voter reactions cost Republicans control of
Congress. Republicans went from 55 of 100 Senate seats to 49 and from
232 of 435 seats to 202 after the elections. The Republican Party had to
accept the voter message and choose what to do next.[19]

Elections and the Communication Process

As an ideal, the combination of parties and elections provides a crude mechanism of communication within a democracy. As elections approach, party leaders consider what they see as important problems. They listen to what voters say are problems. They offer proposals and critique those offered by the opposing party. There is internal debate about what problems are most important and about how they should be addressed. Pundits may offer their wisdom about what is occurring in politics and a diversity of views may cause much internal debate. At the end of the process politicians wait to see what happens in elections.

Once election results come in a party reviews who voted for them and who did not. They review what districts and states were won and which were lost. They form an assessment of whether they got their message across and whether voters agreed with them. If they are the party that won a majority they may conclude they have support for the policies they presented and proceed to take action. If they did not gain a majority they have to take a careful look at what caused their problems. Each party may struggle to interpret all aspects of election results, but they can form a general sense of what motivated voters, or at least their voters, in their vote choice. The interaction of party candidate presentations and the responses of voters convey a sense of what the electorate is thinking. Some rough communication of what voters want is achieved. There are times when political parties in American democracy play out the roles we expect. They create debates, critiques of each other's policies, and voters convey their views.

2   Enduring Doubts about Political Parties

While academics and pundits are generally positive about the role of political parties within the democratic process, many Americans do not share their views about the merits of parties. The doubts do not involve minor quibbles, but fundamental skepticism about whether parties and the politicians who comprise them contribute to democracy. Indeed, there are many who think that political parties ultimately do more harm than help in the political process.

The criticisms are many. The unease begins with doubts about the motives of the people who seek and hold office. Then there is the issue of whether they manufacture conflict that is not there or accentuate the modest differences that do exist. The worry is that in an effort to retain office they seek to create more conflict than really exists. This leads them to focus on presenting distorted information in an effort to scare and mobilize voters and to prompt people to work for and contribute to their campaigns. These efforts to create conflict prompt negative television ads that alienate voters from involvement in politics. The critics do not paint a pretty picture of what parties do to the democratic process.

Ambition and Its Effects

The ideal is that a politician and a political party are vehicles to represent the concerns of the public. Politicians present positions, giving voters a choice about what views they wish to see represented. Politicians are at the center of this ideal. They are the means to achieve representation. A continual criticism of party politicians is that their concern is themselves and not the public. They are seen as ambitious, but largely ambitious for themselves. That ambition is seen as resulting in three very specific problems. First, their primary concern is to stay in office because of the benefits that follow. Second, the desire to stay in office leads them to try to avoid difficult (and sometimes necessary) decisions, which will be seen as controversial and costs them votes. They try to provide benefits to everyone without making choices. Third, the desire to stay in office leads them to "say anything" to please voters. They may not really believe in what they say, but they will say it. Each of these presents the issue of whether we can trust politicians.

The first matter involves the argument that politicians are largely interested in positions because of the benefits that can follow. In 2012 Members of Congress were paid a salary of $174,000 per year. In addition they receive health care and a standard federal pension. They receive funds to run an office in Washington and one in their district, but these funds cannot be taken as personal income. The pay of Members of Congress is well above the national average.[1] For many critics of politicians, these benefits make the position too attractive for its monetary rewards. The charge is that they are more interested in the position than they are in beliefs about what policies should be adopted.[2] As put by one theorist of parties:

> What motivates the political actions of party members. We assume that they act solely in order to attain the income, prestige and power which comes from being in office. They treat policies purely as a means to the attainment of their private ends, which they can reach only by being elected?[3]

In short, politicians propose policies to get elected and do not get elected to propose policies. Their primary concerns are the position and its perks. As they stay in office they become out-of-touch with the average American. The result is considerable antagonism among many voters to career politicians. As expressed by one letter writer: "Our government has, in fact, isolated itself from the realities of daily American life and the struggle to survive. When is the last time our congressional representative paid for their own health care or felt the hardship of unemployment?"

In recent years critics have also expressed concern that the position of being a politician provides too much access to other sources of income. In 2011 a report was released that indicated that 250 of the 535 Members of Congress (435 in the House and 100 Senators) had experienced a much greater increase in their net wealth from 1984 to 2009 than the general public.[4] From 1984 to 2009 the average net worth of Members of Congress increased from $280,000 to $725,056. During that time the net worth of U.S. families went from $20,648 to $20,500. These numbers exclude the value of homes and are expressed in 2009 dollars. The concern is that Members of Congress seek to stay in office because they get access to information about matters affecting businesses, such as regulations and government contracts, which gives them an advantage in investing.

The fundamental anxiety is that the position of being a Member of Congress has become too attractive and for the wrong reasons. More and more Members seek to stay around for lengthy periods of time and they are successful. Figure 2.1 indicates the percentage of House Members who sought and were re-elected over time. Since the late 1800s the success rate of incumbents has steadily increased. Not only are almost all incumbents

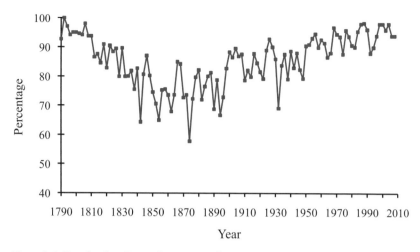

Figure 2.1 Re-election Rates for House of Representatives, 1790–2008.

winning re-election, but beginning in the 1970s many academics became concerned that more and more of them were winning by larger margins.[5] They had taxpayer funded staff to promote them, media consultants to help them present themselves, pollsters to gauge their image, and more campaign money to advertise their accomplishments. The longer they stay the more out-of-touch they become. The concern was that "incumbents have become quite effectively insulated from the electoral effects . . ."[6] Overall, the view of some is not very positive. The larger concern was that House elections were becoming . . . quite unresponsive to shifts in the preferences of voters.[7] The ambitions of party politicians can be harmful to democracy.

Others worry that politicians see elected positions as a means of access to more lucrative jobs after leaving office. Many Members leave and secure positions with high salaries in law firms or consulting firms. They gain these jobs because they have expertise in how Congress works and are familiar with many of the Members and staff. That gives them credibility among businesses and various organizations seeking information on how to approach Congress to have their concerns expressed. Given the various benefits that come from being a Member of Congress, the concern is that people seek and retain the position for the wrong reasons. They are less interested in representing the public than in staying in office long enough to have knowledge of how Congress works so they can land a lucrative position after leaving.

There is also anxiety that careerism and its benefits have made the position so attractive that the pursuit of office is affecting whom politicians listen to and respond to. A Member of Congress needs money for campaigns. They need to hire staff, rent offices, do research, send mail, and produce and run radio and television ads. That takes money. Over the last several decades the cost of campaigns has steadily increased. To obtain the necessary funds candidates turn to those who have more money—lobbyists and the more affluent. The concern is that candidates of both parties have become more responsive to the concerns of those who have the money to fund campaigns. To the extent elected officials are responsive to those who provide these resources that tilts representation to those who have more money.[8]

This unease with career politicians has prompted numerous reforms to contain the presumed negative effects of careerism.[9] Some have sought to make party politicians focus more on the general public and less on the party. Rather than have candidates chosen by party leaders, reformers sought to have candidates chosen by primaries. The presumption is that candidates would have to focus on public concerns and not those of party leaders. Voters would not have the crutch of a party label and would have to assess the individual.[10] In some local governments partisan elections and governments have been replaced by non-partisan elections.

Others argue that any career politician is bad and there should be term limits, or a set number of years a person can be in office. The argument is that if we can create expectations that no one will hold a position for a long time then politicians will focus on doing the right thing for the time they are and then move back into the private sector. Many states and localities have enacted term limits on state legislatures to prevent legislators from turning the position into a career.[11] There have been efforts by states to impose term limits on Members of Congress, but the courts have ruled that states cannot impose this rule on a national institution.

Others have accepted that politicians may serve for a number of years so the focus should be on shaping to whom they respond and how much they can introduce partisanship into government. To make politicians less responsive to those with large amounts of money we have instituted limits on how much any candidate can accept from a donor. All amounts they receive must be disclosed regularly and publicly so the public and opponents can scrutinize where they get their money. The hope is that disclosure will inhibit a politician from appearing to be overly responsive to those with more money.

There is also continual unease about politicians making patronage appointments, or choosing people for administrative positions because of loyalty to the party rather than for their competence. Reformers have advocated for merit appointments and many positions are now civil service appointments, or positions that are filled on the basis of educational credentials and tests. These efforts have been prominent in state and local governments.[12]

Consensus, Social Unity and Creating Political Conflict

While the motives and concerns of party candidates may be seen with suspicion, an equally serious charge is the role they play in creating—some would say manufacturing—conflict. This criticism begins with the argument that we as Americans share some basic values. We believe in limited government and in individualism—leaving people alone to live their own lives, make their own choices, and live with the consequences.[13] Most see America as an exceptional nation.[14] We began without the rigid social strata that dominated Europe. There were no nobility, no aristocracy, and considerable potential for individuals to advance through individual effort.[15] The presumption is that as a result of that legacy Americans share essentially the same values about the nature of our society. We have a consensus.

Given that consensus, ambitious politicians face a challenge. If they are going to create support for themselves and their party, they seek to create differences. As stated by Alexis de Tocqueville in 1848:

> The ambitious are bound to create parties, for it is difficult to turn the man in power out simply for the reason that one would like to take his place. Hence all the skill of politicians consists in forming parties. . . . he is concerned to discover whether by chance there may not be somewhere in the world a doctrine or principle that could be conveniently placed at the head of the new association.[16]

In short, politicians seek out something to create a sense of difference from another party. The charge is that they manufacture conflict that does not really exist. To those who believe there is a consensus of values within American society, parties are vehicles to disrupt that consensus. Rosenblum characterizes these people as having a holistic view of society and notes that "Holists cast parties as parts against rather than parts of the whole."[17] The goal of a party is to create a difference to remove the other party.

Others acknowledge that there are legitimate differences in interests and views in society. They see diversity of concerns and are regarded as pluralists. While they may see differences and conflicts in society, many are not positive about parties. These critics are concerned that parties, in their pursuit of differentiation, seek to accentuate conflict. As James Madison expressed it in *Federalist No. 10* in 1788:

> The latent causes of faction are thus sown in the nature of man . . . we see them everywhere brought into various degrees of activity . . . [by] leaders ambitiously contending for pre-eminence and power [who] have, in turn, divided mankind into parties, inflamed them with mutual animosity, and rendered them much more disposed to vex and oppress each other than to co-operate for their common good.[18]

More than 200 years later, essentially the same sentiments are expressed by political scientist Morris Fiornia, who argues:

> In America today there is a disconnection between an unrepresentative political class and the citizenry it purports to represent. The rhetoric

and activities of the political class reflect a set of issue priorities that are not the priorities of the American public. Clearly, the citizenry as a whole is much less deeply divided between liberals and conservatives than are political elites.[19]

Even some of the politicians in office decry what has transpired. In 2012 Republicans were pushing legislation to allow employers to be able to decline to offer specific health care benefits in their health insurance package if they had moral objections to the benefit. The discussion was revolving around whether contraception for women would be required as an employer benefit in insurance programs. Republicans were seeking to present it as religious freedom while Democrats were presenting the issue as a woman's health care issue and access to contraception. As the vote occurred, Olympia Snowe, a moderate Republican Senator from Maine, surprised many with her announcement that she was retiring. She commented:

> Everybody's got to rethink how we approach legislating and governance in the United States Senate. We've miniaturized the process in the U.S. Senate, no longer allowing lawmakers to shape or change legislation and turning every vote into a take-it-or-leave-it showdown intended to embarrass the opposition.[20]

> We are becoming more like a parliamentary system, where everyone simply votes with their party and those in charge employ every possible tactic to block the other side. I think the American people are in the center in some way.[21]

As the battle over whether employers should have to provide contraception played out in Congress in 2012, a 21-year-old dental hygienist student called the debate a diversion from the real issue of jobs and expressed her dismay about politicians being out of touch: "I am sitting at home eating Raman noodles and everyone in government is eating filet mignon and talking about birth control, and they are all men."[22]

The focus seems to be on intense party showdowns and battles and not resolving problems. Joe Klein, columnist for *Time*, toured the country in September of 2011, and in an article entitled, "Stuck in the Middle: Americans in the Heartland are yearning for compromise while politicians play to the hater," he quotes voters as follows: "The point is, the leaders of both parties aren't listening to us. It's all sensational. Out here, fights like the debt-ceiling crisis over the summer just seem bizarre. It doesn't reflect what we believe."[23]

Using Conflict to Create Support

If parties are creating conflict, why are they doing so? To critics of parties, conflict is created as a means to mobilize voters and resources that will keep the party and its politicians in office. The goals are multiple. First, each party seeks to demonize the opposition in the eyes of the electorate to create anxiety about the other party holding power. A Republican can characterize policies of Democrats as socialism and raise the specter that government is planning on seizing private property. Or they can relentlessly talk about abortion in the hopes that socially conservative working class voters will not think about their economic situation but about how terrible abortion is, and not vote Democratic.[24] A Democrat can suggest that Republican efforts to reform government programs such as Medicare are efforts to elim-inate the program. The arguments from each side have a hint of the demise of something of fundamental importance if the other side attains power.

These efforts at shaping and perhaps distorting perceptions are enabled by changes in the media. From the 1950s to the 1970s there were three major networks, many strong local newspapers, and no internet or cable. That meant most voters received somewhat the same information. Since then cable shows have become much more pervasive and important as a source of information. The internet has become a major source of information for many. Viewership of the "evening news" has declined dramatically.[25] Increasingly, a person with strong partisan views can watch cable shows that reinforce her biases. She can go to websites that present "facts" that may not be accurate. There is now a greater occurrence of self-selection in sources of information.[26] These sites can be used to present interpretations of what the other party is doing that alarm the base of the party.

As an example, a poll in 2010 found that the percentage of the public thinking that President Barack Obama was a Muslim had increased from 12 percent in 2008 to 18 percent in 2010.[27] He is not a Muslim but is a Christian. The presumption is that these voters were acquiring information from internet sources or conservative media outlets. The phenomenon is not confined to one party. In 2011 Republicans in the House of Repre-sentatives voted to change Medicare to a voucher system or one in which individuals received a subsidy to buy their own insurance on the market. The subsidy amount would be less than the current spending per person in Medicare. The Republican argument was this would encourage people to be more concerned about costs and usage and help hold down the growth in national Medicare spending. Very quickly liberal outlets were saying that Republicans had voted to end Medicare. While their proposal might reduce benefits, it would not end the program.

If this anxiety can be created among many voters, then it can be used to generate support among those voters.[28] Loyalists can be bombarded with emails claiming the other side has nefarious plans to change policies. Party supporters will then be more inclined to donate money to the party. MoveOn regularly sends those on its email lists notices that Republicans are seeking to do terrible things and donations are urgently needed to counter their efforts. Democrats then benefit. Each year in January a conference is held in Washington of those opposed to abortion. Those at the conference claim that abortion is increasing and those opposed need donations to fight to limit abortion.[29] Republicans then benefit. Those activated will be more likely to work for candidates of the party and to turn out and vote for candidates of the party. Each party has a base of probable supporters and the concern is to keep them engaged and motivated to support the party.

Criticisms of the other party are often used as efforts to mobilize that base. For example, in explaining the logic of the 2004 presidential re-election campaign of President George W. Bush, Karl Rove, his political advisor, indicated that he thought getting Democrats to vote Republican was unlikely. His plan was to find and mobilize Republicans.[30] It has become common to hear of many campaign managers focusing on "mobilizing the base." That means convincing the base that the alternative will be very bad. That in turn leads to language that creates a stark contrast and a greater sense of conflict.

The fundamental issue is the presumption of how much the public is divided. Some argue that the divisions in the public are no different than they were in the past. Opinion on various abortion policies has not really changed, but politicians are now intensely divided.[31] In this view the problem is not the public but the politicians: "Perhaps the public are the grownups in this account, and the temper-tantrum-like behavior of our political elites is just so much sound and fury. They may, that is, signify nothing."[32]

Distorting and Alienating the Public

The hope of many is that democracy can be a process of citizens talking through issues and policy proposals and reaching some sort of accommodation.[33] To many the most serious problem with partisanship is that politicians are more interested in distorting the dialogue to increase support for their side. Parties are seen as more interested in shaping how an issue is seen as a means of mobilizing voters than having a debate and resolving problems.[34] As a part of alerting voters to the dangers of the other party acquiring power candidates and parties regularly use speeches and negative ads to present us with unflattering portrayals of policy options and candidates. We are told opposing candidates engage in unethical practices, that they vote against our interests and for some "special interests" that want policies harmful to the rest of us. These efforts have two significant impacts. In the short term, attacks—particularly negative ads—can be very effective in increasing the extent to which candidates are seen unfavorably. In the jargon of campaigns, they "drive up the negatives" of candidates and can reduce the support for the candidate attacked.

The fundamental concern is that parties have become so effective in negatively portraying the other side that evaluations of candidates and social conditions are increasingly driven by voter partisanship. A Democrat sees a Republican president in negative terms and a Republican sees a Democratic president in negative terms. That has probably always occurred, but the impact of partisanship in evaluations has increased in recent decades. This is evident in the differences in job approval of presidents of Republican and Democratic voters. If 70 percent of Republicans approve of a Republican president and 50 percent of Democrats approve then the difference in approval by party is 20 points. If 80 percent of Democrats approve of a Democratic president and 40 percent of Republicans approve then the difference is 40 points. From the 1950s through the George W. Bush administration (2001–2008) this difference grew from about 40 percent to 80 percent.[35] For much of the Obama presidency the difference has been 60–70 percentage points.[36] The concern is that in forming judgments voters are using information less and just forming their judgments based on the partisanship of the politician.

As an example of how partisanship can affect voters, a poll conducted in 2004 asked voters whether President George Bush intentionally exaggerated evidence about Iraq having weapons of mass destruction before the U.S. invaded the country. The results are below. What is interesting about the question is the word *intentional*. No voter could know whether George Bush intentionally made statements misleading voters. Despite that, 76 percent of Democrats thought he did, while only 30 percent of Republicans did. This was very likely a case where partisanship so affected people that it affected the inclination of Democrats to believe something about intentionality.

The impact of partisanship now goes well beyond the reaction to candidates. It appears that partisanship is affecting an array of perceptions of society (Table 2.2). In 2000 Democrat Bill Clinton was president and during 2001 George W. Bush was president. As partisan control of the presidency shifted to a Republican administration, Democrats became remarkably less optimistic about their finances, while Republicans changed much less. Democrats apparently perceived that a Republican president would hurt them.

Table 2.1 Reactions to George Bush by Party, February, 2003[a] (percent within each group answering yes or no—sum down)

	Democrat	Independent	Republican
Did Bush intentionally exaggerate evidence that Iraq had weapons of mass destruction?			
Yes	76	56	30
No	23	42	66

a   *Washington Post*/ABC News Poll, "Bush Faces Rising Public Doubts on Credibility and Casualties Alike," *Washington Post*, July 10, 2003. http://abcnews.go.com/images/pdf/929a1BushIraq.pdf.

Table 2.2 Partisanship and Perceptions

	Democrat	Independent	Republican
Are you optimistic about your personal finances? (Percent optimistic – percent negative)[a]			
October 2000	43	36	19
February 2001	28	7	24
June 2001	–9	2	21
August 2001	–22	3	11
Change	–65	-33	–8
Consumer confidence (November 2006)[b]			
Getting better	20	37	73
Getting worse	75	56	22
Has economy begun to recover (January 2012)[c]			
Has	66	40	23
Has not	30	58	74
Do you think the federal government poses an immediate threat to the rights and freedoms of ordinary citizens, or not? (September 2010)[d]			
September 2006	57	50	21
September 2010	21	49	66
Change	–36	–1	45

a Lydia Saad, "Gallup Consumer Indicator Turns Negative for First Time Since 1993: Declining confidence may reflect partisan politics as well as economic concerns," August 30, 2001: www.gallup.com/poll/4837/Gallup-Consumer-Indicator-Turns-Negative-First-Time-Since-1993.aspx.
b Lydia Saad, "Is Consumer Confidence More Politics Than Economics? Republicans and Democrats give vastly different ratings of nation's economy," November 2, 2006: www.gallup.com/poll/25303/Consumer-Confidence-More-Politics-Than-Economics.aspx.
c *Washington Post*, "President Obama faces stiffly divided electorate to start fourth year in office": www.washingtonpost.com/politics/president-obama-faces-stiffly-divided-electorate-to-start-fourth-year-in-office/2012/01/17/gIQAwEkp6P_graphic.html.
d Jeffrey M. Jones, "Republicans, Democrats Shift on Whether Gov't is a Threat: Republicans more likely to view government as threat now, Democrats more likely in 2006," October 18, 2010: www.gallup.com/poll/143717/Republicans-Democrats-Shift-Whether-Gov-Threat.aspx.

When asked whether the economy was getting better or worse in 2006 (under Republican President George W. Bush) Democrats were very negative and Republicans were very positive. When asked whether the economy was getting better or worse in 2012 (under Democratic President Barack Obama) Democrats were very positive and Republicans were very negative. Voters were asked in 2006 and 2012 whether the federal government was an immediate threat to freedom. In 2006, 57 percent of Democrats said yes, but with Obama as president only 21 said yes. In 2006 21 percent of Republicans said yes, but with Obama as president 66 percent said yes.

The concern is that how voters respond appears to be significantly influenced by their partisanship and which party holds office. While parties do pursue policies that may help their base more than the other, it is hard to imagine actual policy changes and effects that could create such differences and changes in perceptions. It is difficult to have a democratic discussion when partisanship is significantly affecting perceptions of the world. As former Senator Daniel Patrick Moynihan is reputed to have said "Everyone is entitled to their own opinions, but they are not entitled to their own facts." If partisanship creates different perceptions of facts then discussion is difficult.

There is evidence that these partisan criticisms and attacks alienate voters who dislike all the negative information.[37] As voters listen to all of the negative ads some come to dislike campaigns so much that they just tune them out and decide not to vote. The worry among critics of the political parties and their politicians is that they have become less worried about governing the nation and more worried about staying in power. They then engage in criticisms that exaggerate and distort facts. They oppose the other party reflexively and pursue a game in which their primary concern is to embarrass the opposition.[38]

Frustrations of the Public

We are now witnessing protracted policy conflict in Congress with each party seeking to stymie the other. The public in turn, far less divided than party elites, develops very negative views of political parties.[39] Over the last two decades Gallup has found that as many as 50 percent of voters have a negative view of each party.[40] This in turn affects judgments of government. Voters have also been asked for 60 years whether they trust government in Washington to do the right thing just about always, some of the time, or never. We generally combine the responses to the first two and treat these as "trust government." In the 1950s and 1960s between 60 and 75 percent of respondents indicated they trusted government. Since then the percentage has declined and now ranges from 20 to 50 percent. What is of great concern is that over the last decade, as partisan conflict has steadily increased, trust has fallen steadily from 50 to 20 percent by 2010.[41] Approval of Congress reached a new low of 11 percent in December, 2011, as partisan squabbles persisted across the entire year.[42] As partisan conflict has escalated in recent years the public has become less positive about how the nation is governed.[43]

The cumulative effect of all these matters is considerable unease about political parties. In the twenty plus years from 1988 through 2012 Gallup found that the percentage identifying as Independent increased from 33 to 40 percent.[44] Central to this unease are doubts about the role played by career party politicians. The concern is that they prolong conflicts as a means to mobilize their electoral base. In the Fall of 1995 the House of

Representatives was held by Republicans. They wanted large budget cuts and President Bill Clinton resisted. The eventual result of the showdown was a temporary shutdown of government. The conflict was seen by the public as excessive partisan squabbling.[45] In the summer of 2011 Congress was faced with the issue of raising the debt limit—the amount the government is authorized to borrow and pay back—and the deadline created another showdown in which it appeared the United States might default on its debt to borrowers for the first time in history. Polls indicated that a majority of the public wanted political leaders to compromise.[46] Only at the very last minute default was avoided and the debt limit was increased.

The ideal between how we think political parties can contribute to democracy and what much of the public thinks of parties is significant. The critics do not paint a pretty picture of what parties do to the democratic process. Indeed, they argue that the current partisanship is poisoning the political process, pitting party members against each other when it adds little to the process. Indeed, it creates hostilities that make it difficult to get anything done. As reporter Ron Brownstein summarizes it, we can't make any progress on social problems because:

> the day-to-day functioning of American politics now inhibits the constructive compromises between the parties required to confront these problems. The political system has evolved to a point where the vast majority of elected officials in each party feel comfortable only advancing ideas acceptable to their core supporters, their base (10). Political leaders on both sides now feel a relentless pressure for party discipline and intellectual conformity ... (11). Voters on the losing side always feel unrepresented when the other party wins unified control over government (19).[47]

It is not a portrayal of politics comforting to many voters.

Part II

Parties and Political Conditions

3 Notions of Party and Conflict

The criticisms of political parties are serious and trouble many people. Together they suggest that parties are more concerned with posturing and retaining offices than with representing the public and responding to problems. It is hard to watch contemporary politics without having these reactions. The discrepancy between the ideal and realities of party behavior is real and troubling. They trouble some people so much they have tried to create alternatives to party politicians, such as the direct referendum presented to voters or the creation of independent public authorities to make decisions.[1]

Despite these efforts, parties remain central to American politics. Parties, for good or bad, are the vehicle for responding to social change and representing concerns. We need to understand why the ideal does not play out as clearly as we might presume. To the extent we do not understand how they work and whether they contribute to democracy we will be uneasy and disappointed in democracy.

The argument to be presented here is that while the behavior of parties is often puzzling and frustrating, their activities in many ways make sense. Five matters are important to understanding why parties act as they do.[2] First, a party is far less of a coherent and hierarchical entity than is often presumed. The internal disputes that occur and the range of actors involved in shaping party direction often result in the party being ambiguous about its position on some issues. Second, they are continually struggling to understand the precise nature of their electoral base, how they achieved it, and what they should emphasize in the current election. Third, neither party has a majority, meaning they must consider who can be attracted to achieve a majority. Fourth, as they pursue efforts to create a majority coalition they face a society that is continually changing. Assessing those changes and deciding how to react leads to internal debates, protracted disputes and indecisive and shifting positions. Fifth, they operate before an electorate that often pays only limited attention and through a media that is continually changing and often does not convey the content party members wish. That affects how they present positions. Together these conditions create continual uncertainty about what positions they should adopt, how their positions will be received and whether unexpected events will occur that may disrupt their plans and require them to shift direction. This uncertainty means they often misjudge the public's reactions and are forced to adjust.

Together these five matters make it very difficult for a "party" to choose positions. They make the presentation of positions more simplistic than many might like. They lead to shifts of positions that many find odd and puzzling. Their behaviors, however, make sense, if we incorporate the impact of the conditions just reviewed. The resulting party behaviors may not be "rational" in the eyes of some, but they are explainable. The argument is that, given the conditions they face, they do as well as might be expected. The primary goal of the remainder of this book is to explain how the conditions that parties face, prompt much of the behavior we see. In explaining their behavior, the concern is to respond to the criticisms presented in the prior chapter.

The Nature of a Party

The usual definition of a party is that it is a collection of like-minded individuals who seek to win elections to control government to enact the policies they support. Very often, though not always, the focus of this definition is on the formal party organization and its actors—the candidates and elected officials, the state and national party organizations, and the congressional campaign committees. These actors are seen as the people who devote their energies to recruiting candidates, raising funds and helping with campaigns.

This presumption that a party is defined largely by elites, formal organizations, and their activities has been the basis for conclusions that parties declined in the 1960s. As primaries became the means of choosing candidates, parties were seen as losing control of who represented the party. This was furthered by the growing ability of challengers and incumbents to raise their own funds, hire their own pollsters, design and air their own commercials, and run their own campaigns.[3]

The focus on formal organizations is far too limited a definition of a party, however. The party might best be thought of as a network of actors with policy preferences seeking to influence nominations, strategy, policy emphases, decision-making, and image. All share the goal of pushing the party in a policy direction and winning a majority. The actors may be elected officials at all levels, non-elected party officials at all levels, actual and potential donors, candidates seeking to run, interest groups, activists, consultants, and those willing to work for the party if it goes in the direction they wish. They may be seen as part of a more formal organization[4] or as part of the enormous group of people and organizations that can provide support, whether that be philosophical encouragement, workers, mailing lists, or donations.[5] There may be considerable disagreement among all these actors, with each arguing and maneuvering to get their viewpoint adopted as the party focus. Who among all these actors is relatively more important can vary from time to time as the party struggles with what image it should project.[6] It is an informal network with diverse actors seeking influence.

The significance of this notion of party is that there is often less unity of views within a party than we might presume. Its positions may be unclear and unsettled as issues and policy directions are argued over. Its positions may also be gradually changing as one set of activists push the party in a new direction.

Conflict: Substance or Posturing?

Perhaps the most important issue in seeking to make sense of what a party is and who comprises it involves what they are seeking to represent. Are they representing significant differences or are they essentially exaggerating differences as a means to acquiring power? Are there real issues being contested in America and do the growing political divisions of recent decades reflect a growing divide? There are very different interpretations about this issue. Sorting them out is crucial for understanding what motivates party actors and how they approach presenting their positions to voters.

There are essentially two different views about the extent of conflict in American society and politics. One side argues that Americans are not really that divided while the other argues that conflicts are real and about fundamental matters. The first view is that Americans have always shared the essential values of individualism and limited government.[7] Most Americans do not know much about politics and are moderates.[8] They are not agitated about many of the issues that consume elected party politicians. The distribution of political opinions is about the same for many issues now as it was several decades ago. To the extent there are greater divisions between the political parties in Congress it is largely because elites are polarized. Their polarization is because they are "disconnected" from the American public and perhaps creating differences to keep themselves in power.[9] The elites are seen as caught up in the insular ways of Washington and creating more conflict than exists.

While that view is embraced by many, the presumption of this book is that there are real conflicts.[10] The argument that there are not significant divisions has three major flaws. First, it poses the issue in a simplistic way that misses the way conflict emerges. It presents the issue as an either–or proposition. The nation is seen as either divided or not. There has probably always been a large portion of the public that is moderate, or relatively uninformed, or not engaged in intense discussions about political issues. Many people are busy living their lives and wrapped up in other things. Conflict can emerge because of mass activism, but the more common way is that activists, opinion leaders, and political candidates assess the state of society and government and react.[11] They see an issue as important and begin to try to make that issue part of the public agenda.

In the 1950s and 1960s civil rights issues were pushed by activists who felt an injustice had gone on long enough.[12] In the 1980s and 1990s social conservatives became more active and pressured candidates because they thought the social trends in America—abortion, crime, out-of-wedlock births, welfare dependency—were increasing at disturbing rates and represented a decline in adherence to responsible behavior standards. In the last decade there has been an increase in arguments that inequality is increasing and is detrimental to society. On the other side are conservative activists arguing that social "entitlement" programs are growing too fast. Programs such as Medicare, Medicaid, and Food Stamps automatically provide benefits to anyone qualifying and critics argue they are consuming too many tax dollars. They also argue that the costs are rising and creating a situation where the federal government has to borrow money to pay for them. This is leading to greater government debt.

The activists on both sides of issues struggle to get the attention of elected officials. They form interest groups and raise money to try to mobilize those sympathetic. Sometimes they succeed in putting an issue on the agenda and other times they do not. When they do succeed the issue gets more and more attention and may become an issue that each party must consider either as something they must deal with or as presenting an opportunity to appeal to voters. Even as this process continues much of the electorate may only gradually focus on the issue and form judgments. Candidates, activists, and the media may increasingly focus on some issues, but much of the public may be inattentive. At any one time some are intense and divided, others are somewhat attentive, and others are not paying any attention. The divisions come from those most attentive. Posing the question as whether the nation is divided or not misses how political issues emerge and become part of the debate. Some are intense about issues and many are not. It is those who are concerned that are important.

Second, the argument that we are not divided or at least no more so than in prior decades confuses the distribution of opinion with how it is organized into party groups. Parties structure the debate. The issue is whether parties represent groups of people who are internally similar and differ considerably from the other party. The parties were not as divided in the 1960s and 1970s. In the decades since then conservatives have become more concerned that government has become too intrusive, regulating and taxing too much, and diminishing the role of individual initiative and responsibility. They saw increases in the size and scope of government, in the growth of welfare rolls, in tax levels, and in crime and abortion, and felt the need to react and try to reverse those trends. Liberals have very different concerns. They have grown more concerned about differences in equality of opportunity, inequality in the distribution of income, concentrations of economic power, and social limits on those who choose to live differently than the majority wishes.[13] These differences became motivation for activists and party members to organize and seek to attract those who agree with them. Their goals are to create a larger party electoral base that agrees with them and use of the party as a vehicle to influence government policies. Each party has increasingly staked out clear positions and attracted supporters who agree with the positions being presented by the parties.[14] The lengthy process of seeking to attract more like-minded voters has brought the Republican Party more conservatives and the Democratic Party more liberals.[15]

An indication of changes occurring in American politics is shown in Table 3.1. People have been asked in national surveys whether they see themselves as liberal, moderate or conservative since 1972. While the term has different meanings to different people and we should interpret it with caution, it provides a rough indication of what is happening to shape the nature of conflict. The first two columns sum down and indicate the percentage of the public choosing a label, or declining any category. Over 36 years the distribution of liberals, moderates, conservatives, and no choice has been relatively stable. That is the basis for the argument that there has not been change within the electorate.

The important matter, however, is how these people are organized by party. The next set of columns sum across and indicate the party identification of liberals and conservatives in 1972 and 2008. In 1972 there was already a clear pattern that most liberals (70.4 percent) saw themselves as Democrats and most conservatives (55.9 percent) saw themselves as Republicans. As the parties have clarified their positions and pursued voters the percentages of liberals choosing the Democratic Party has increased. Likewise the percentage of conservatives choosing the Republican Party has increased. The result is that conflict has become more organized. There is more of an "us versus them" nature of conflict.[16] The result is that conflict is accentuated. The partisan arguments are more focused and more intense when there is greater unity within each party.

Table 3.1 Aligning Liberals and Conservatives, 1972 and 2008

| | Ideology (sum down) | | Party Identification by Ideology (sum across) | | | | | |
| | | | 1972 | | | 2008 | | |
	1972	2008	Rep	Indep	Dem	Rep	Indep	Dem
Liberal	18.5	21.1	19.6	10.1	70.4	7.5	6.2	86.3
Moderate	26.9	22.2	34.4	12.8	52.8	22.7	17.2	60.2
Conservative	26.5	27.1	55.9	10.5	33.6	65.2	6.8	28.0
No choice	28.1	29.5	27.5	21.2	51.3	14.7	15.5	69.8

Source: NES cumulative file, 1948–2008.

Third, there are reasons to see the differences and conflicts as more serious because of the connection among issues. That is, a person who holds a liberal opinion on one issue increasingly holds liberal opinions on other issues. Conservatives follow the same pattern. Ideologies have become more consistent. This has created more unified and opposing views of problems and what policies should prevail.[17] Views on issues of race, proper social norms, and economic situations have become related, increasing the sense of difference between those with opposing views. Those who see racial injustice are also more likely to be concerned about economic inequality and support government social programs. They are more likely to see government as an actor that creates an environment that maximizes individual opportunity *and* freedom. They are more likely to support access to abortions and believe gays should have the same rights as others. In contrast are those who may see differences in how people fare by race, class, and sex, but believe strongly that social mobility exists and the emphasis in American society must be on individual initiative and responsibility if the society is to prosper.[18] They believe that there are clear rules of how life should be lived and that members of society should follow those rules.[19] Abortion is seen as immoral and reflects personal irresponsibility. Social programs are detrimental because they create an entitlement mentality that undermines personal responsibility.[20] Over time these different sets of views have come to be seen as comprising alternative ideologies of how society works and what policies should be adopted.[21]

How this has come about is still being studied. In some cases those with specific opinions found the party they were identifying with was shifting its positions. Over time people resolved this conflict by moving to identify with another party.[22] In other cases party identifiers listened to arguments and adopted opinions in line with their party. Party elites have sought to present arguments that views about capitalism and individual rights and responsibilities are connected[23] and there is evidence that some party identifiers have accepted these arguments and moved to adopt positions the party is presenting.[24] Regardless of how it has developed, opinions on various issues now have a higher association. The process of attracting and losing various voters has taken decades, but partisan attachments are increasingly divided by race,[25] class,[26] ideology,[27] and religious attachment.[28] Within Congress Democratic and Republican legislators are increasingly divided.

The parties now represent real conflicts over what norms and values individuals should follow, how much government should involve itself in our lives, whether government should help those less well-off or reduce the burden on those successful, what taxation levels should be imposed, what role religion should play in society and how should government be related to religion, and many other matters. Republicans argue for more emphasis on individual initiative, less of a role for government, and more respect for a public role for religion and its moral codes. Democrats have taken positions more sympathetic to those who have less opportunity and struggle in life. They see government as a vehicle to address these issues, and they are uneasy about religion being too entangled with government. The important matter is that the conflicts we are seeing are not manufactured. They reflect real and deeply felt beliefs about American society.

Ambition and Representation

These conflicts frustrate much of the public. They think that the ambition of politicians to create a career in Congress or a state legislature leads most of them to accentuate and exaggerate conflict. They do so to inflame and mobilize sympathetic groups to support them so they can stay in office. The presumption is that amid all the conflict that exists there is some sort of consensus on policy, a public interest, a common ground, and that should be the focus. If only we could get more of them to "do the right thing."

Democracy, however, involves the principle that the people are to be listened to. Their concerns are supposed to be paramount. If voters have different and strongly held notions of what policies should be adopted, then those views should be represented. If someone thinks the poor are at a serious disadvantage in terms of opportunity and that equality of opportunity should be a defining trait of American society,[29] then those views need to be represented. If someone else thinks that the poor do not work hard enough and have poor work ethics, and that federal assistance will enable and support bad personal practices, then those views need to be represented.[30] That is, there may not be a consensus and there may be serious conflict within American society. There may not be a common ground. The challenge for democracy may be to debate these alternative notions of what will make a society fair and work well, and come up with the best compromise it can.

If there are real differences we want someone to represent and advocate for them. The best mechanism found thus far is to rely on politicians who want to get re-elected. While it is valuable to have a politician who is similar to the people within his district, it is the ambition to stay in office that makes a politician be attentive to his or her constituency. It is ambition that makes a politician listen closely to the passions of constituents and wonder how many others share those views. They worry about how plant closings, recessions, and new and old programs affect people in the district. They wonder how important abortion and gay rights issues are. Ambition makes them sensitive because they don't want to lose.

Their sensitivity may lead them to change their views as they sense that opinion in their district is shifting. Presidential candidates have to listen to the public and many of them have to shift their opinions. Even Ronald Reagan, often seen as a true conservative, recognized the need to adjust. He remained true to many conservative principles but he did shift in some opinions. Many Democrats recognized over time that unlimited access to welfare was increasingly being seen very negatively by the public and that Republicans were casting them as the party of the "hand-out." Many recognized the shift in opinion and many agreed to reform welfare in 1996 and limit access to two years at any one time and five years over a lifetime. Republicans were adamantly anti-gay until they recognized that public opinion was changing and becoming more accepting. They then changed to favoring equal rights for gays but not gay marriage.[31] Politicians seeking re-election generally listen to voters.

Term limits, while appealing to many, will remove that incentive. Politicians might seek to present the concerns of their constituency because they share their beliefs, but the connection becomes chancier. Term limits will probably make legislators think more about their next job than representing their constituency. Term limits create more turnover, remove the expertise of veteran legislators, and make politicians more reliant on interest groups and the executive branch for information. For good or bad, the re-election drive is the best means of attaining representation.

That does mean that ambitious politicians will not disappoint many critics. These same ambitious politicians may exaggerate issues. They may do so to raise money and mobilize supporters. They may do so because they sincerely believe in their positions. In seeking to represent particular interests they may posture beyond what many of us would like. Their positions may not be sincere in the sense of reflecting their own views. But they are the vehicles to make sure that the concerns of voters in a district or state are listened to and made a part of debate. To the extent that a party is comprised of those who share similar beliefs, the combination of ambition and beliefs will result in the representation of those beliefs as the process of making policy decisions evolves.

In summary, parties are arguing about fundamental issues. They represent voters with differing views, though with considerable variation in the intensity of their views. The parties are presenting differing visions of what norms should be honored and what policies should prevail. Even if this perspective on parties is accepted, the behavior of parties still frustrates many. They seem to simplify and posture more than is necessary, to change their stances and make people wonder about their positions, and to engage in belligerent exchanges that make having policy discussions difficult. They balk at compromising and create impasses while social problems persist.

The question is why they engage in these practices and do their behaviors contribute to the democratic process. The parties have different electoral bases and seek different policies. But they also face considerable uncertainty in just how to position themselves. The five political conditions mentioned at the beginning of this chapter are crucial. First, it is not clear realignment is over. Second, there are different interpretations of what created realignment. Third, no party has a majority. Fourth, social change is continuing. Fifth, much of the electorate is disengaged and the media are fragmented. These conditions contribute to uncertainty and create some behaviors that puzzle and annoy voters. The next several chapters attempt to elucidate how political conditions explain why they engage in these behaviors and how the parties still contribute to the democratic process.

4   Shifting Electoral Bases

As any campaign begins a party first assesses their electoral base. Which voters do they consistently attract? Which states does their presidential candidate win and where does it win House and Senate seats? The first political condition that affects parties is that there has been enormous change in American politics over time in the regions where each party receives its primary support. How much different groups vote Democrat or Republican has changed. As change occurs this presents each party with the question of whether their base is clear and whether change has ceased. Are the changes of recent decades complete? Have they produced a solid base for the party? Might further gains among some groups be likely in some areas if the party positions itself properly?

At the beginning of the 1900s the political divisions in America were fairly clear. Democrats dominated the South and Republicans dominated the North. Republicans were the majority party, while Democrats were the minority party and struggling to attract voters outside the South.[1] Eventually the Great Depression occurred and Republicans chose to respond minimally. Democrats became the best alternative and they received a majority while making significant inroads outside the South.[2] The party worked very hard to retain this new base and was able to create a coalition of southerners and urban immigrants and union workers that dominated American politics for the next 30 years.[3] Eventually Democrats acquired such a strong majority following the 1964 elections that they were able to enact a large number of social programs such as Medicaid and Medicare.[4]

While the Democratic dominance of American politics seemed fairly stable in the early 1960s, it was during this decade that major and sustained changes occurred in the geographical electoral bases of American political parties. The story is an involved one, but it can be summarized as follows. Issues of how to treat blacks, how many programs the federal government would support, and what kinds of personal behavior would be encouraged by government policies began to divide the society. The parties were beginning to head in opposite directions on race issues, with Republicans arguing that there were limits to how much government should intervene in such matters.[5] The conservative movement had started to develop in earnest in the 1950s, but during the 1960s it became more prominent with the nomination of conservative Barry Goldwater as the 1964 Republican presidential nominee.[6] Many in the party saw the South as more conservative and thought that despite the presumption that the South was committed to the Democratic Party, it could be converted to the Republican side.[7] At the same time many northern Democrats were frustrated with the conservativism of the southern base and wanted to put more emphasis on winning the North.

These efforts to transform the electoral bases of the parties were lengthy, but they eventually did change from where each party drew its strongest support. The concerns of the different regions were shifting and changing what people in each region wanted from government. The North was relatively liberal, pro-unions, supportive of policies such as abortion and civil rights.[8] The South moved significantly more Republican over several decades.[9] The North and particularly the Northeast moved away from the Republican Party and became much more Democratic.[10]

The transitions in partisan loyalties of the regions[11] of the nation are presented in Figures 4.1 and 4.2. From 1900 through roughly the 1950s the South remained solidly Democratic while the rest of the nation was solidly Republican. Then change began and by the 2000s the partisan support for the regions had reversed. The South is now the strongest Republican base and the North is now the strongest Democratic base. The change has taken a considerable length of time but it has occurred.

The important matter is what this process of change has meant for party actors. As these changes occurred, the association across House districts between presidential and House results declined. Beginning in the 1960s a Republican presidential candidate might do well in a set of districts but Republican House candidates might not do well. The partisan vote in a

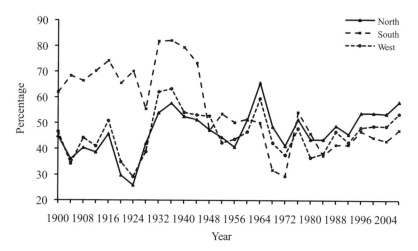

Figure 4.1 Average Democratic Presidential Vote by Region, 1900–2008.

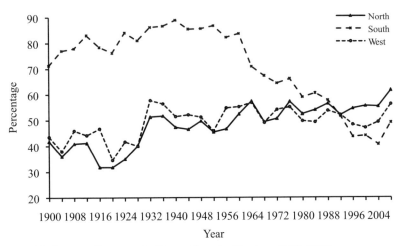

Figure 4.2 Average Democratic House Vote by Region, 1900–2008.

House district could diverge considerably from that for the president. If so, a Democratic presidential candidate might win the district but a Republican House candidate might win the House seat. These cases are known as split-outcomes. Figure 4.3 indicates the correlation between presidential and House results and the percentage of House districts with split-outcomes. During the 1960s through 1980s the correlation declined and split-outcomes increased.

These changes over the 1960s–1980s created a general sense that parties did not mean as much and that candidates were largely conducting campaigns and presenting themselves rather than a party to voters.[12] For parties and candidates the implication was that working together and presenting a unified policy image was a chancy strategy. Party actors were being presented with an interpretation of elections, which suggested that party meant less. Each candidate should accept that it was best to operate independently.

The reality is that this interpretation, plausible as it seemed at the time, was mistaken. How presidential and House candidates were faring in regions of the nation was changing, but they were changing at different rates. That created the impression that election results were becoming disconnected. Presidential candidates were able to improve their vote percentages in some regions before their House candidates could. Many House incumbents wanted to remain in office and resisted changing their positions to adapt to the shifting concerns of their party. Conservative House Democrats survived for some time in the South while Republican presidential candidates won the district. Liberal to moderate House Republicans survived in the Northeast as Democratic presidential candidates won their district. Gradually, House Members in these districts retired and were replaced by Members from the other party. The result (Figure 4.3) is that the association

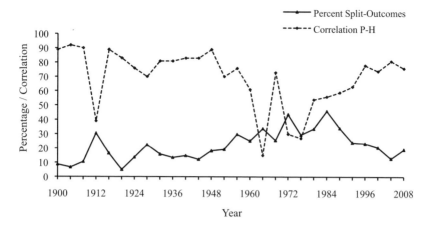

Figure 4.3 Presidential–House Election Results, 1900–2008 Elections, all Districts.

between presidential and House results increased and the percentage of split-outcomes House results declined.[13]

Mixed Implications

As presidential–House election results came together the notion of a party as presenting a unified policy position by presidential and House candidates becomes more plausible. Voters are now more inclined to vote at the same levels for presidential and House candidates than they did 30 years ago. Voters who identify with a party are now voting for their party candidates at higher levels than in prior decades.[14] With a common electoral base it made more sense to act as a party and not as separate candidates.

As tempting as that revised interpretation is, both parties know they still have to be cautious. In the 2000s there were still between 13 and 21 percent of House districts with split outcomes. The average divergence in vote percentages between the presidential and House partisan vote was still over 10 points during the last decade. Each party must operate with the knowledge that some of their congressional members are in office because they have created or benefited from a partisan vote in their district that was different than the presidential candidate received. There is more party voting now than in recent decades, but there is still some divergence within districts and a party must recognize that in considering how much of a unified image to present. It is unknown whether the future will bring presidential and House votes closer together or will some separation be possible for House candidates. Change creates uncertainty and it is not clear yet whether change has ceased and we are now in a situation where the geographical bases of each party are relatively stable.

The result of the uncertainty about whether political coalitions are stable is that parties often vacillate in their positions. They think that a part of the coalition is settled and stable, but then a position is taken and poll results suggest that some part of the coalition does not like the position. The most loyal part of the party base may like the position, but others may not. Then a party has to adjust and de-emphasize the position, much to the disappointment of the most loyal base. Uncertainty creates vacillation.

5 Conflicting Interpretations of Change

The political parties now have different geographical bases than they did 50 years ago. Conservatives are more inclined to identify with the Republican Party and liberals with the Democratic Party. In some ways it appears people have largely sorted themselves out between the two parties and each party has a clear base and knows what issues to stress. However, for those actually engaged in politics and thinking about what issues to emphasize it is not simple what should be done. Anyone consulting the vast array of academic studies and political commentary available would encounter remarkably conflicting interpretations of what issues created the realignment just reviewed. These differing interpretations are important because they provide explanations of what created change. To the extent that politicians embrace an interpretation of what created change they may well assume that the same factors will reinforce existing divisions or create even more change. If someone argues that X has caused Y and those changes improved the fortunes of a party, then a party seeking a majority may conclude it is best to stress X in the upcoming elections.

The problem facing party strategists is that the interpretations differ and in fundamental ways. While there are many confident arguments about what has created change, each study is challenged by another that argues that another factor is driving change. In what follows no attempt will be made to arbitrate among the diverse interpretations. Discerning truth is elusive. What is important for understanding party behaviors is to realize the diversity of interpretations party strategists must wade through in deciding what is influential in shaping electoral alignments.

The Party Decline/Candidate Centered Interpretation

In the 1960s through 1980s there was a decline in the association between presidential and House election results (Figure 4.3). The percentage of House districts with a split-outcome steadily increased and by 1984 was 46 percent. The percentage of the electorate indicating they were independent was rising (Figure 6.1 in the next chapter). To many, something had changed in American politics. The old economic divisions were seen as fading in relevance. The parties differed less than in prior eras. Members of Congress were acquiring more resources to present themselves to voters as individuals.[1] Polling was becoming available along with direct mail companies with the ability to find and send mail to likely voters.[2]

The logical conclusion was that issues mattered less as an explanation of changing electoral patterns. Candidates were operating independently of whatever party image existed. The result was an outpouring of studies suggesting that parties were declining[3] and that campaigns were becoming focused on candidates.[4] The logical implication for party strategists was that candidate campaigns should be conducted separately. The focus should be on raising money and saturating the public with images of how much the Member of Congress has done for the district.[5] Given this interpretation it did not make much sense for a party to formulate and present a unified policy stance to the electorate. The evidence for this interpretation is increasingly doubtful and of limited value in explaining the current polarization.[6] Regardless, the interpretation is still very much alive.[7] Anyone reading current academic works on campaigns will encounter the argument that campaigns are candidate-centered.[8] If all this is the case, then candidates may well want to be careful how much they are associated with the national party image.

Attracting (and Losing) Voters

Other interpretations have a very different focus. These begin with the presumption that parties are seeking to attract voters that they think will be compatible with their general principles and might help them achieve a majority. They also presume that many voters have moved from one party to the other so there is a need to understand what moved them. To attract new voters a party must identify voters currently attached to another party, but who are unhappy with one or more of their party's positions. These are conflicted voters, or cross-pressured. They agree with their party on some issues and disagree on others. The trick is to focus on the issues that trouble them to pull them away from the other party.[9] These issues are often called "wedge" issues, or ones used to drive a wedge between the voter and her party. The disputes in interpreting changes in American politics involve what issues have motivated changes in party loyalties. With all the polling data that exist, you might think that resolving this issue should be possible. The reality is that analysts bring their perspectives and convictions to their analyses and it is usually possible to find some evidence for their view of what is driving change. Again, it is not possible to arbitrate the many claims made. Indeed, the point is not to arbitrate them but to indicate the range of arguments presented to political strategists.

To simplify, the arguments about what is creating change boil down to two competing claims. One argument is that economic issues and class divisions were once dominant but they have faded in relevance in recent decades. Assuming that is accepted, the question becomes what has displaced these issues. Some argue that race has become the dominant division and has pushed aside other sources of division. Others argue that the issues troubling the public are broader and involve cultural matters—what values should be honored, expected, and supported. If the interpretation that economic issues matter less is accepted, then party candidates should focus on how they discuss and legislate about values. In contrast, others argue that, with inequality growing and economic security issues paramount, economic issues and class divisions have not declined. In fact, they have increased, and more and more conflict revolves around the policies that affect the distribution of opportunities, income, and wealth. To anyone reading the diversity of offered interpretations of what is shaping political divisions in America there are no clear answers. Each deserves a brief overview to provide some sense of what is encountered.

Race

In the 1950s the Democratic Party derived a substantial portion of its electoral base in Congress from the South. There were signs their grip on the South was slipping and the northern wing of the party wanted to pursue liberal policies.[10] The Civil Rights movement was growing stronger and challenging the segregation and repression of the South. President Lyndon Johnson and the northern contingent of the Democratic Party (along with many Republicans) staked out a clear position in favor of several Civil Rights bills, and began the transformation of the party to having an image as favorable to minorities.[11] This brought the party much greater support among Blacks and more support within the North.

This was a time when the Republican Party began to move to a more conservative position on issues seen by many as related to race. The party was pursuing a Southern Strategy, which meant emphasizing its opposition to greater power for the federal government to intervene in state affairs.[12] It also meant expressing its strong opposition to riots, crime, and welfare at a time when urban riots were occurring, crime was increasing, and welfare rolls were increasing. To some the central issues driving change in American politics are expanding opportunities for minorities and the reaction of whites to those efforts.[13] The argument is that Democrats became too sympathetic to minorities and this created resentment among whites, and particularly among working class whites who felt threatened by more competition for jobs and did not want housing integration.[14]

The evidence typically presented to verify that Democrats are losing whites is along the lines of Figure 5.1. Over the last 60 years white men have moved from being predominantly Democratic to Republican. If the argument is accepted that Democrats are driving away the white working class, then stances on race issues are crucial and the Democrats may have to be careful about looking too sympathetic to minorities.[15] There are

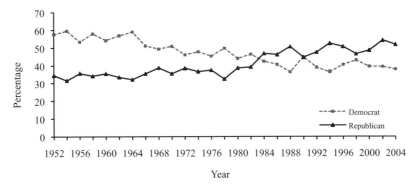

Figure 5.1 Party Identification (with Leaners) for White Men, 1952–2008.

plausible challenges to this interpretation, as will be discussed shortly, but the important matter is that there are many studies that conclude that race is the central issue shaping American politics and any party strategist has to at least consider this explanation of what is happening.

Cultural Issues

The other major explanation of why economic issues have declined in relevance—assuming they have—involves the impact of cultural issues. These involve issues of what is moral or proper behavior. Beginning in the 1960s and 1970s crime began to rise, along with divorce rates and births out-of-wedlock. In 1974 the Supreme Court declared abortion legal and reported abortions began to increase.[16] Gays were also pushing for repeal of many laws that denied them the same rights as heterosexuals. Many of these trends were disturbing to those with a belief in traditional norms. They saw the emergence of an indulgent lifestyle in which individuals were less responsible for their actions. The general presumption was that the greatest concern came from those with less education who were less tolerant of differences in how people lived.[17] Those with less education were more authoritarian or inclined to believe they should adhere to the traditional standards of the society.[18]

These differences in concern about eroding cultural norms became politically relevant when Republicans began to stress their concern about cultural issues. The argument of conservatives within the party was that capitalism should prevail and that this should take place in a society that follows traditional notions of disciplined, moral, and responsible behavior.[19] Republicans were able to emphasize these issues to those with less education and draw them away from the Democratic Party. By pulling them away they reduced the Democratic base and provided less of a base from which Democrats could focus on economic issues. Because of the greater concern of the working class with cultural issues and the strategy of the Republican

Party, the focus on economic issues was diminished and Republicans had more leeway to change tax laws to benefit the affluent.[20]

Given this interpretation, Democrats were advised to put more emphasis on being tough on crime, not accepting out-of-wedlock births, hedging on gay rights, and not advocating for abortion but being "pro-choice" so the issue was the right of women to make their own choices. By some accounts the nature of issues central to American politics had changed and the shift favored Republicans.[21]

The Unresolved Relevance of Class

Whether the important factors are race or cultural issues, these interpretations have resulted in an interpretation that economic issues are no longer as relevant or potent. Perhaps the most important matter for those trying to understand what was shaping debate in American politics was the argument that class divisions had been displaced by cultural divisions. Some argued that changes had been so dramatic that class divisions were inverted. The more affluent were voting Democratic and the less affluent, angered by race favoritism, resentment of elite dismissal of their culture, and issues such as abortion and gay rights, were voting Republican.[22] It soon became accepted that class was not a significant source of division.[23] Those claims were then absorbed by journalists and commentators. David Brooks, a columnist, stated "The Republican Party is the party of the white working class. They overwhelmingly favor Republicans."[24] Reporters

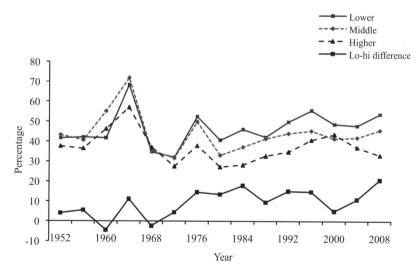

Figure 5.2 Democratic Presidential Voting by Income Groups, Whites Only, 1952–2008.

assessing electoral prospects for an upcoming presidential race often state "In recent elections, blue-collar white voters have been overwhelmingly in the Republican column."[25] Given these interpretations, parties might presume that their most important focus should be on understanding the cultural positions of voters.

To some these conclusions seem hard to believe. Inequality is increasing and those in the bottom half of the income distribution are experiencing very few gains in income and in the accumulation of wealth. There is also evidence that the conclusion that class has become less relevant is inaccurate. Figure 5.2 groups white voters by whether they are in the top, middle, or bottom third of the income distribution and indicates what percentage within each group voted Democratic for president for each year since 1952.

The patterns are enough to create some puzzlement about what is happening. Several matters are important. First, there is considerable volatility in voting Democratic over time, making any long-term interpretations based on any particular election of questionable value. Second, many presume the New Deal coalition that Democrats relied on in the 1950s and 1960s was based on a relatively strong vote from lower income whites. The evidence indicates there was little difference during the 1950s and 1960s between the lower and higher third in support for Democrats. Third, perhaps the most intriguing matter is that support for Democrats among whites in the lower third has gradually increased since the 1960s and 1970s. Their difference from higher income whites has also increased.[26] The data trends contradict the interpretations that class divisions were once great and that they have declined. The evidence suggests just the opposite. It is enough to leave a political strategist puzzled about what studies indicate.

Further, anyone studying American politics would think that studying only whites excludes a growing percentage of the American electorate. As will be discussed later, the percentage of Americans who identify as white is gradually declining. While each party may have a clear base, they do have to face the reality that not just whites are voting and as the non-white component of the electorate grows they have to think how issues will play out before that changing electorate. That raises the question of, if we are trying to decide whether class matters, shouldn't the entire electorate be considered? Figure 5.3 presents results for all voters, again grouped by thirds. The patterns over time are essentially the same, but at higher levels because non-whites vote more Democratic. The patterns shown are not different if voting for the House of Representatives is examined.[27]

For someone trying to assess how much economic issues matter, the interpretations just reviewed make their task difficult. It is further complicated by another argument. Almost everyone who approaches the issue of class focuses on how the working class is behaving. Neglected in all this is how the upper education and income groups are reacting to these debates. Some appear to presume that they all want lower taxes and fewer social programs. But those with more education and more income may see a

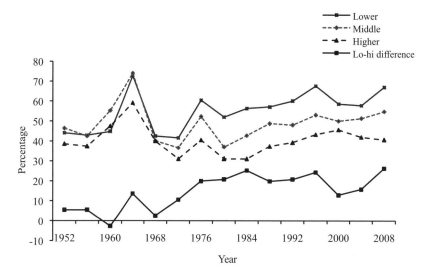

Figure 5.3 Democratic Presidential Voting by Income Groups, All Voters, 1952–2008.

cultural focus as reflecting intolerance of others. And this may make them uneasy. David Brooks has argued that:

> over the last few decades, the Republican Party has driven away people who live in cities, in highly educated regions, and on the coasts. The big [reason] is this: Republican political tacticians decided to mobilize their coalition with a form of social class warfare. Democrats kept nominating coastal, pointy-heads like Michael Dukakis so Republicans attacked coastal pointy-heads. The nation [became] divided between the wholesome Joe Sixpacks in the heartland and the over-sophisticated, over-educated, over-secularized denizens of the coasts. Republicans developed their own leadership style. If Democratic leaders prized deliberation and self-examination, Republicans would govern from the gut. The Republicans have alienated whole professions. It has lost the educated class by sins of commission—by telling members of that class to go away.[28]

If Figures 5.2 and 5.3 are examined, there is no pattern of those in the upper third moving away from the Democratic Party. Indeed, in some years they moved more Democratic. There is also evidence to support Brooks' claim that upper income voters who are liberal on social issues (and many are in that category) are more likely to vote Democratic.[29] All this suggests that the Republican emphasis on social conservative views may not be moving the working class to the Republican Party and they may be losing some voters.

Implications

Sorting out these different interpretations is not just an academic matter. That is, it is not just something for academics and commentators to squabble over while those involved in politics watch with a mixture of curiosity and bemusement. These are arguments about what matters to voters and what moves them to identify with a party. They involve issues of what a party can stress to voters and gain their support. They also involve issues of how much either party has to worry about responding to the economic or cultural positions of the other party. What has been reviewed here is just a "tip of the iceberg" of the volume of books, reports, newsletters, and essays that regularly emerge. Each provides an interpretation of what has happened, what is likely to occur, and what a party should do to achieve a majority. Many are confident and assertive, and often with limited data. The result of the net outpouring is that it is difficult for party strategists to have certainty about just what explains change and what they should do.

The result is that parties are often tentative in their proposals, trying out one idea based on one explanation of what drives voters and then waiting to see who it attracts and who it loses. It often results in indecisive parties, which many voters do not like.

6   The Lack of a Majority

A party is a loose network of actors who have some commonality of beliefs and who seek to be in power to enact the policies that reflect their beliefs. A fundamental political condition that presents a challenge to a party is whether they are operating from a majority or minority position. If a party has support from the majority, then candidates can continue to express the policy positions and support the same legislation that they have in prior years. If a party is in the minority, the actors face the issue of whether to be satisfied with that status and presenting their views or do they want to derive a strategy to seek to achieve a majority.[1]

The problem facing parties in American politics is that it is not clear if either party has a majority. Each party can find evidence to justify a claim that they represent more voters than the other. But there is also contradictory evidence and that creates considerable uncertainty and debate about what the party should do. Is its base close to a majority and should it focus on mobilizing the base? Or is it in a minority and should it seek to attract those who claim to be independent?

The situation of the parties has varied considerably over time. In terms of winning offices there have been periods where one party dominated. From 1900 to 1932 Republicans had a clear majority. Then from 1932 through the mid 1960s Democrats had a clear majority. From 1968 through 1994 Republicans won most presidential elections but Democrats dominated Congress. Then in 1994 Republicans won control of the House and from 2000 through 2006 Republicans held the presidency, the House, and generally the Senate.

The current situation presents a significant challenge to each party. By some measures neither party has a majority. One indicator is the percent of the population that identifies as a Democrat or Republican. People are asked in surveys whether they see themselves as a Democrat or Republican, Independent, or something else. Those who do not indicate whether they are Democrat or Republican are asked whether they lean to either party. We might also add leaners to those initially indicating an identification to gauge the total extent of partisan support because studies indicate those leaning to a party vote much like self-proclaimed partisans.[2] Figure 6.1

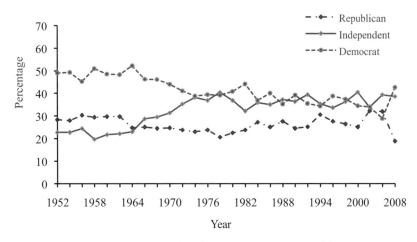

Figure 6.1 Percentage of Voters Identifying as Democrat, Republican, or
         Independent, NES Data, 1952–2008.

indicates the percentages initially choosing each party or declining to choose
a party from 1952 to 2008. Figure 6.2 indicates the percentage of party
identifiers if leaners are added in.

   The results in Figure 6.1 suggest that neither party currently has a
majority. Democrats had a bare majority until 1966. Since then their identifiers have declined and by the 2000s neither party had a majority identifying
with one party. Democrats might argue that there are many "closet
partisans" and that if leaners are included as partisans then they are close to
having a majority, as Figure 6.2 indicates.

   Determining how many voters support a party is made more difficult
because data indicate that partisan identification fluctuates over time. The
Gallup Poll regularly asks respondents to indicate their party identification.
In recent years they have also asked whether those initially indicating they
are independents lean to either party. Their results for the last two decades
are presented in Figure 6.3. Democrats may occasionally reach the point
of being able to claim that 50 percent of the public supports them, but it
does not last. These data indicate each party faces a challenge in getting a
majority of the electorate to identify with them.

   These data can be challenged, however. There are always other data and
those seeking to understand their party's extent of support look at diverse
data.[3] While party identification can be seen as relatively equal, it is also
the case that surveys indicate there are considerably more conservatives than
liberals in America. Figure 6.4 presents the Gallup Poll's results from the
last two decades. There are consistently about 40 percent that identify as
conservative and 20 percent that identify as liberal. It is very easy for a conservative to assume that America is far more disposed to favor conservative
policies than liberal ones. Further, as Table 3.1 indicated, many conservatives

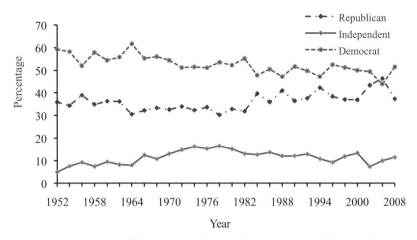

Figure 6.2 Percentage of Voters Identifying as Democrat, Republican, with Leaners Added, NES Data, 1952–2008.

do not now identify with the Republican Party.[4] The reaction to these data among some conservatives is to argue that the party should define itself more clearly as conservative so they can attract those conservatives still identifying with the Democratic Party. If they do so, they could be closer to being the majority party. Their sense is that there are many conservatives who just have not made the transition to being Republican.

Tempting as that interpretation is to Republicans and conservatives, there is also considerable evidence that many Americans say they are conservative, perhaps in principle, but they do not want a lot of the social programs that exist cut.[5] As some have concluded after reviewing a great deal of survey

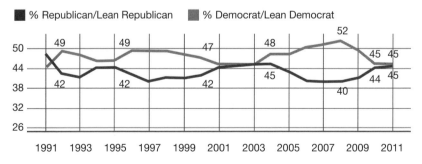

Figure 6.3 Party Identification (Including Independent Leanings), Annual Averages, Gallup Polls, 1991–2011.

Note: Gallup began regularly measuring independents' party leanings in 1991.

Source: Jones, "Record-High 40% of Americans Identify as Independents in '11," Gallup Poll; Russell J. Dalton, *The Apartisan American: Dealignment and Changing Electoral Politics*, (Washington, D.C.: CQ Press, 2012), 11–30.

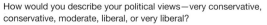

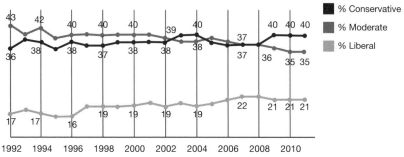

Figure 6.4 U.S. Political Ideology—1992–2011 Annual Averages.
Note: Based on 20 Gallup and USA Today/Gallup polls conducted in 2011.

data, Americans are conservative in the abstract but liberal in practice. Voters say they are conservative, but most do not want cuts in Medicare, federal aid to local schools, grants to attend college, assistance for the poor, or environmental enforcement. Data are not simple in what they convey about how the public is reacting to party principles and arguments. It is by no means clear what the majority position of Americans is and no party can claim a clear majority for its positions.

Election Results

Given the disputes about what are majority views within the public and how many support each party, the next matter to assess is election results. They are often seen as what Americans really support. Politicians continually question polls and say only November matters. As true as that is, the meaning of election results is not always clear. It sometimes appears that party members often see what they want to see in results. The essential difficulty is deciding whether results can be taken as a reaction to proposals in the campaign. Party candidates present their policy proposals during a campaign. They very often assume that voters listened closely and either embraced or rejected the proposals. If the party secures a majority they may well assume that they have a mandate to pursue the proposals they presented.

It is rarely that simple, however. We have repeated cases of the interpretation following an election being questionable. In 1964 Republicans ran Barry Goldwater, a committed conservative, as their presidential candidate. The electorate rejected him and his party and provided Democrats with the presidency and substantial majorities in Congress. The party interpreted their majority as a mandate to enact numerous liberal programs. In the years following that there was considerable speculation that the party had over-reached and there was not a strong mandate for a liberal agenda. In 1980 Ronald Reagan was elected president over sitting President Jimmy Carter. Many interpreted Reagan's victory as support for moving in a conservative direction. It was equally plausible that the election was a rejection of a president presiding over high inflation and high unemployment. In 1994 Republicans, led by Newt Gingrich, took control of the House of Representatives for the first time since 1954. Gingrich took the victory as a mandate to curtail government spending and threatened to shut down government unless President Clinton (Democrat) agreed to change the budget according to his wishes. The public turned against Republicans and Gingrich had to compromise with President Clinton. It was plausible that the vote for Republicans was really a reaction to Clinton's effort to expand the provision of government funded health care in 1993–94 and not an endorsement of the agenda Gingrich was proposing. In 2006 Democrats regained the House of Representatives and concluded this indicated strong support for curtailing the war in Iraq. They soon found it was probably more of a negative reaction to George Bush and the management of the war than a sense that America should just pull out. It is never easy to discern just what a significant electoral swing means.

The situation of the last decade provides no support for the idea that either party has a majority. Table 6.1 presents the results of presidential and House elections across the decade of the 2000s. Using the 435 districts drawn for the 2000s and averaging Republican presidential vote percentages for the three elections of 2000, 2004, 2008, the table first indicates the distribution of the average Republican presidential vote. During the decade Republican presidential candidates averaged 55 percent or more in 149 districts. They averaged less than 45 percent in 165 districts. Neither party could claim a majority of districts in which their presidential candidate averaged a relatively safe percentage. There were 121 districts where the average was close enough to 50 such that a good or bad year for the party could produce a win or loss for the party in those districts. Further, some of the districts that averaged less than 45 percent for the Republican went over 50 percent during the decade, and some of the districts that averaged over 55 percent for the Republican dipped below 50 percent during the decade. Not only does neither party have a majority of reliable districts, but there is volatility in voting.

Not only does neither party have a reliable majority of House districts that their presidential candidates win, but the same is true for House candidates. Table 6.1 indicates (row "all") the percentage of times Democrats won a district 0, 1, 2, 3, 4, or 5 times out of the 5 elections held 2002–10. Democrats won 38.6 percent of districts 5 out of 5 elections. Republicans won 37.2 percent of districts 5 out of 5 elections (or in the table Democrats won 0 of 5). That is, neither party has a majority of House districts they can always count on winning. Each has about the same reliable base.

Table 6.1 Democratic Partisan Seat Success in the House by Republican
        Presidential Votes, 2002–2010 (Out of 5 Elections)

Presidential Average[a]	N	% of Districts	Percent of Times House Seat Won by Democrat (sum percentages across to 100)					
			0	1	2	3	4	5
All	Sum down		37.2	8.3	5.3	3.5	7.1	38.6
<45	165	37.9	.6	.6	1.2	2.4	4.2	90.9
45–49	46	10.6	26.1	13.0	19.6	6.5	10.9	23.9
50–54	75	17.2	50.7	18.7	6.7	8.0	9.3	6.7
55 +	149	34.3	74.5	10.1	4.7	1.3	8.1	1.3

a It is possible to obtain the Republican presidential percentage in 2000 for the 2002 district
  configuration. This is taken from CQ Press' *Congressional Districts in the 2000s: A Portrait
  of America*. They took the results from 2000 and re-tabulated them for the new districts.
  The results for 2004 and 2008 are then averaged with the re-tabulated results to give three
  presidential results for the same district.

The ability of each party to win in districts is closely tied to how their
presidential candidates do. In those districts where Republican presidential
candidates averaged less than 45 percent, House Democratic candidates won
all five elections in 90.9 percent of those 165 districts. When Republican
presidential candidates averaged over 55 percent, Republicans won all five
elections in 74.5 percent of those 149 districts. The challenge for each party
is to win the districts (121 of them) in between. Again, no party has a clear
majority.

State and U.S. Senate election results provide another indicator of
whether either party has a majority. Table 6.2 first again indicates how
Republican presidential candidates fared in states for the three elections of
2000, 2004, and 2008. Republican presidential candidates averaged 55
percent or more in 17 states and less than 45 in 14 states. Neither party has
a majority of states in which their support is strong. There are 19 states that
are in between and it is in those states that candidates must compete to
win. Then there are Senate partisan outcomes and their relationship to
presidential results. Senators serve six year terms, so the turnover is less.
Members may not be up for election in a year their party does poorly, so
they can survive while the state turns against their party. Table 6.2 assesses
which party held seats (two per state) over time regardless of when elections
were held. In only 24 percent of the states did Republicans hold all seats
over the five elections (or Democrats held it 0 times). In only 18 percent
of the states did Democrats always hold the seat over the five elections.

As with the House, there is a relationship between how a state votes for
presidential candidates and which party holds Senate seats during the decade.
In states where a Republican presidential candidate averaged less than
45 percent, Democrats held the Senate seat most of the time. When a

Table 6.2 Democratic Partisan Seat Success in the Senate by Republican
Presidential Votes, 2002–2010 (of 5 Elections; 2 Senators per state,
maximum of 10 times Democrats could hold seats in a state)

	N	% of States	\multicolumn{5}{c}{Number of Elections Senate Seat Held by Democrat}
			0	1–3	4–6	7–9	10
All	Sum down		24.0	12.0	20.0	26.0	18.0
<45	14	28.0	7.1	0	0	42.9	50.0
45–49	10	20.0	0	30.0	40.0	20.0	10.0
50–54	9	18.0	22.2	11.1	33.3	22.2	11.1
55 +	17	34.0	52.9	11.8	17.7	17.7	0

Republican presidential candidate averaged 55 percent or more, the Senate
seat was generally held by a Republican. It is the states where the average
was between 45 and 55 that no party has a clear advantage.

Implications

There is considerable commentary about the polarization of American
politics and how the parties in Congress have stubbornly staked out very
different positions. Despite that, each party is not in a position in which it
has a solid base that allows it to focus only on its core base. Each party faces
an electorate in which no party has a majority that identifies with it. It does
not have a majority of states that consistently support its presidential
candidates. It does not have a set of House districts or Senate seats (states)
that constitute a consistent majority.

This situation creates uncertainty and some erratic behavior for parties.
They must assess what is of concern to voters and what issues they must
address if they are going to win a majority. It affects how they present
themselves to voters. They sometimes are concerned about responding
to their base because that base provides their strongest support. The base
provides contributions, either from individuals or interest groups. The base
provides volunteers for campaigns. But that base is inadequate for winning elections. To garner a majority they have to move beyond their base
and appeal to those more moderate. The example discussed earlier of the
issue of which employers would have to provide contraception coverage
is an example of when the handling of an issue becomes erratic as a party
balances the desires of its base with the search for a majority. Republicans
in Congress expressed strong opposition to the mandate announced by the
Obama administration that institutions operated by religious organizations
would have to provide coverage for contraception. Their base saw this as
government infringement on religious freedom, but many moderates were
uneasy with denying women this coverage. The party eventually decided

to pull back and reduce the focus on their stance as they sensed that to moderates economic issues were more important than this issue.[6] Parties often vacillate between the two appeals as they try to decide what will work in each particular election cycle. There is a process of trial and error in the search.

YBP Library Services

STONECASH, JEFFREY M.

UNDERSTANDING AMERICAN POLITICAL PARTIES:
DEMOCRATIC IDEALS, POLITICAL UNCERTAINTY AND
STRATEGIC...   Paper   135 P.
NEW YORK: ROUTLEDGE, 2013

TITLE CONT: POSITIONING. AUTH: SYRACUSE UNIV.
ASKS WHETHER PARTIES SERVE PUBLIC INTERESTS.

LCCN 2012-12711
ISBN 0415508436   **Library PO#** GENERAL APPROVAL

		List	34.95	USD
		Disc	10.0%	
5461 UNIV OF TEXAS/SAN ANTONIO		**Net**	31.46	USD
App. Date 10/03/12 POL.APR	6108-11			

SUBJ: POLITICAL PARTIES--U.S.

CLASS JK2265   DEWEY# 324.273   LEVEL GEN-AC

YBP Library Services

STONECASH, JEFFREY M.

UNDERSTANDING AMERICAN POLITICAL PARTIES:
DEMOCRATIC IDEALS, POLITICAL UNCERTAINTY AND
STRATEGIC...   Paper   135 P.
NEW YORK: ROUTLEDGE, 2013

TITLE CONT: POSITIONING. AUTH: SYRACUSE UNIV.
ASKS WHETHER PARTIES SERVE PUBLIC INTERESTS.
LCCN 2012-12711

ISBN 0415508436   **Library PO#** GENERAL APPROVAL

		List	34.95	USD
		Disc	10.0%	
5461 UNIV OF TEXAS/SAN ANTONIO		Net	31.46	USD
App. Date 10/03/12 POL.APR 6108-11				

SUBJ: POLITICAL PARTIES--U.S.

CLASS JK2265   DEWEY# 324.273   LEVEL GEN-AC

7 Continuing Social Change and Events

The ongoing process of realignment and the lack of a majority within the electorate make policy positioning a challenge for parties. To add to their uncertainty, social change creates two more sources of anxiety. First, the society that parties are trying to represent is continually changing. The nature of jobs and economic conditions change. Inequality in the distribution of income increases. Unions and manufacturing decline. Abortion is declared legal by the Supreme Court. Legal and illegal immigrants increase as a percentage of the electorate. The cost of social programs grows. Federal debt increases. Gays become more aggressive about seeking rights. Parties have to continually monitor the society they face. They have to decide whether to form a reaction to these changes and present that to voters.

Sometimes changes are more abrupt and their significance is hard to anticipate in advance. When Hurricane Katrina struck the Gulf coast in 2005 few realized how the response to it would affect the reputation of the Bush administration. In 2009 the Obama administration was presented with the issue of how to respond to the financial crisis. Each presented a juncture that would affect a party's image.

Second, there is the uncertainty of how voters will react to these changes. Will inequality become an issue and how much will it, if at all, divide voters? Will immigration bother voters, how many, and which ones? Are the growth of social programs and debt seen as tied together? How much do voters really care about debt? Who wants cuts and who opposes them? A conservative or liberal politician has to decide whether the issue is important, who is on what side and how to talk about the issue. The extent of social change and how the electorate will react present continual challenges to parties. The following presents some examples of changes that present parties with a significant challenge about how to respond.

Growing Inequality

From the mid 1940s through the early 1970s inequality in the distribution of income declined. Individuals at all income levels experienced increases and those at the lower levels grew more than others, reducing differences between those at the top and bottom.[1] Then in the 1970s the trends reversed. Inequality began to steadily increase. Studies regularly documented that most gains in income were going to those already making high incomes. The accompanying chart, from a Congressional Budget Office study published in 2011, indicates the shares of income held by quintiles (fifths) of the population in 1979 and 2007. Over this time period those in all quintiles except the top one received smaller percentages of income. This was because their increases in income were small or modest while those at the top received large increases.[2] Inequality in the distribution of wealth has also increased over time.[3]

The important matter for party leaders is whether this inequality is likely to become a political issue. Is growing inequality seen as a result of impersonal forces that individuals must just cope with in an increasingly competitive world or is it a product of manipulation of political and economic conditions. There are strong advocates for each interpretation. On one side are those arguing that the American economy is changing within the world economy and individuals have to adapt. Manufacturing plays less of a role and creative service activities are far more important now. The American economy is now tied in with the global economy. Economic activity moves around according to where markets are and the necessary labor can be found. Those who are educated and have the skills to compete in this changing economy will do best. Our policies should stress encouraging individuals to secure education to adapt to change.[4] Redistributing income will not solve the problem and further taxation of the more affluent is unfair. The top 10 percent of tax filers are paying 70.5 percent of all income tax revenue and the top 25 percent are paying 87.0 percent.[5]

Others provide a very different narrative of how this inequality developed. The alternative interpretation is that conservatives and the affluent mobilized over time to change the rules of the game to create this shift. They funded think tanks to produce studies supporting the value of capitalism. They sought to change the tax system to favor those with large investments. Capital gains, or money made from investing, became taxed at lower levels. Other provisions of the tax law were changed to favor the affluent and tax rates for the affluent were lowered. Efforts were made to constrain the ability of unions to raise wages or companies were moved to states where unions have less influence.[6] Inequality did not just happen, but was engineered.

The inequality trends and the two competing narratives present a potential problem for each party. They must assess how many people are aware of these trends, whether they troubled by them, which interpretation is getting through to voters and which is being accepted. Even if one is accepted more than the other, do voters think there is a solution to the trends?

The difficulty party strategists face is that as they consult poll data, the results are conflicting. There are poll results that indicate that people worry

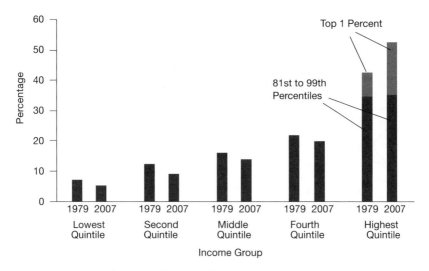

Figure 7.1 Shares of Income after Transfers and Federal Taxes, 1979–2007.

about the extent of inequality and they think that income should be more evenly distributed.[7] There are polls that indicate that an increasing percentage of Americans see conflict between the rich and the poor.[8] But there are also poll results that indicate that a majority of Americans think the economic system is fair to them.[9] They may see inequality but poll data indicate that they are more worried about having an opportunity than resenting the rich.[10] When asked "Do you think what you achieve in life depends largely on your family background or on your abilities and hard work?" in a 2004 poll, 60.8 percent said hard work and abilities and 7.4 percent said family background.[11] The public clearly has conflicted opinions about inequality.[12]

It is not clear how opinion on this issue will develop in the future. If inequality continues to increase, Wall Street executives continue to receive large bonuses, and the economy does not create more middle-income jobs, inequality could become a major political issue. The dilemma for each political party is whether to take a stand on the issue with all its risks. If Democrats try to make it an issue and the public sees that as redistribution that is against American values, it could hurt. While Bill Clinton was president he tried to emphasize providing opportunity and not redistribution with a slogan of "A hand up, not a hand out." If Republicans choose to ignore the issue and inequality does become an issue they could be seen as uncaring and insensitive. But if their constituency sees their success as a result of hard work, they do not want to see their party emphasize more taxes and benefits for others. It is not clear how each party should respond to the inequality issue.

Immigration

The composition of American society is changing and it creates uncertainty about how each party should respond to change. America experienced steady and significant immigration in the late 1800s and early 1900s. That prompted considerable opposition and in the 1920s Congress enacted several laws sharply curtailing further immigration. Then in the 1960s Congress chose to allow for more immigrants. In recent decades immigration has steadily increased the percentage of the U.S. population that is foreign-born and in 2007 it was 12.6 percent, the highest percentage since 1910.[13] Figure 7.2 indicates how the percentage foreign-born has changed over time.

These immigrants present a challenge to many Americans. Many do not speak English and they bring their culture from their country with them. This is seen by many as a threat to American culture.[14] The unease about immigration has been accentuated by concerns about the number of illegal immigrants. It is estimated that there are now between 11 and 12 million illegal immigrants in the United States.[15] The influx of immigrants, and particularly Hispanics, is changing the political composition of many states. As Hispanics locate in states along the southern part of the United States— from California to Florida and in the states above that—the parties are facing a shifting population. These are states that Republicans once thought would be solidly Republican.[16]

These changes are evident in House districts and in states. Table 7.1 indicates the distribution of House districts by their percentages of non-whites from the 1960s through 2011. The data on districts drawn for the 2012 election are not available at the time of writing this. In the 1960s 22.0 percent of House districts had 20 percent or more of non-whites. By the 2000s almost one-half of House districts (49.4 percent) had 20 percent

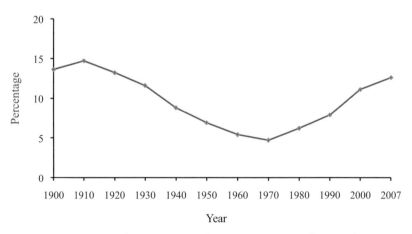

Figure 7.2 Percentage of American Population Foreign-Born, by Decade, 1900–2007.

Table 7.1 Distribution of House Districts by the Percentage Non-White
1960s–2000s

% Non-white	Decade of Apportionment and Percent Distribution				
	1960s	*1970s*	*1980s*	*1990s*	*2000s*
0– 9	64.8	61.9	44.8	40.2	23.2
10–19	13.1	18.4	24.8	24.6	27.4
20–29	9.4	7.4	15.4	16.8	19.3
30 plus	12.6	12.4	14.9	18.4	30.1

or more non-whites. The districts drawn for 2012 on the basis of the 2010 census will show a further increase.

The changes in the population are also evident in data from the states. Table 7.2 indicates the situation for states, grouped by regions. The Census Bureau conducts a census every 10 years and asks individuals to indicate their ethnicity or race. In a report from March 2011 the Census Bureau groups all those who are not "non-Hispanic white alone" into "minority." The census began to allow individuals to indicate multiple identifications in 2000 so the same questions were presented in the two years. The former consists of all of those who identify only as white. The important matters are what changes have occurred and where have they occurred.

From 2000 to 2010 the "white alone" population grew very little (Table 7.2), increasing by 1.2 percent. In contrast, the "minority" population increased by 28.8 percent. Furthermore, the greatest changes occurred where Republicans thought they would have a strong base, the West and the South.

Table 7.2 Percentage of Population Non-White, by Region, 2000 and 2010 (population in 1,000s)[a]

Region	2000			2010			% Δ 00–10	
	Total	*Minority*	*Percent Minority*	*Total*	*Minority*	*Percent Minority*	*White*	*Minority*
Northeast	53,594	14,267	26.6	55,317	17,309	31.3	–3.4	21.3
Midwest	64,392	12,006	18.6	66,927	14,830	22.2	–0.6	23.5
South	100,236	34,309	34.2	114,555	45,849	40.0	4.2	33.6
West	63,197	26,286	41.6	71,945	33,939	47.2	3.0	29.1
Nation	281,421	86,869	30.9	308,745	111,817	36.3	1.2	28.8

a   Karen R. Humes, Nicholas A. Jones, and Roberto R. Ramirez, *Overview of Race and Hispanic Origin: 2010,* U.S. Census Bureau, March 2011: www.census.gov/prod/cen2010/briefs/c2010br-02.pdf; and, "Racial Composition Change by CD," Swing State Project: April 12, 2011: http://swingstateproject.com/diary/8688/racial-composition-change-by-cd.

These changes present a political challenge for both parties. The unknowns are whether this minority population will register and vote and how will they vote.[17] In recent years Hispanics have tended to vote Democratic, so Democrats might assume that an appeal of sympathy and understanding of their plight in getting started in America might generate greater votes from this growing group. That has potential drawbacks, however. Many within the minority group are immigrants and they take a while to become naturalized citizens, registered and politically engaged enough to get to vote. Many also have lower incomes and less education, which typically is associated with lower registration and voting rates. Appealing to the immigrant portion of this population might not pay off politically. Finally, many whites see immigrants as disruptive to America culture. Others see minorities as undeserving and think Democrats are too sympathetic.[18] The issues for Democrats are whether the non-white population will show up and vote Democratic and whether too much of an appeal will drive away whites.

Republicans have their own uncertainties to deal with. Some of their base sees minorities as taking jobs and consuming too many social services. Appealing to that sentiment, however, has its risks. Many businesses—manufacturing, service, and agricultural—rely on legal and illegal immigrants for workers. While some might sympathize with unease about "different" Americans, they need workers and are not interested in efforts to police businesses for whether all their workers are legal. Further, there is a serious risk in the Republican Party appearing to be intolerant at a time when the minority population is increasing as a percentage of the electorate. Democrats have been willing the Hispanic vote. Some Republicans believe that the party has a message of ambition and individual achievement that could very effectively appeal to immigrants who came to America to improve their lives. Criticizing the culture of immigrants and their children will not win their support. Appealing to their ambitions and economic concerns might.[19] The difficulty is part of the Republican base is hostile to immigrants and minorities and the party has to decide how to satisfy this base while creating a message and image that will help the party in the future.

Cultural Issues: Gay Rights

Much has been made of the role of cultural issues in recent years. The argument is made that Republicans have become skilled in using issues such as opposition to abortion and gay rights to appeal to those in the working class who are more authoritarian and attached to traditional patterns of living.[20] The logic is that they can use these cultural issues as a "wedge issue" to pull a voter away from their "normal" voting pattern.[21] A lower income person might be supportive of Democrats for their position on trying to address issues of equality of opportunity, but conservative on other "cultural" issues. They are what we call cross-pressured—pulled in different directions in their partisan support by differing opinions. To the extent that

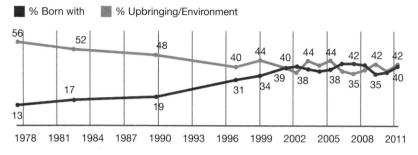

In your view, is being gay or lesbian something a person is born with, (or) due to factors such as upbringing and environment?

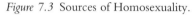

Figure 7.3 Sources of Homosexuality.

Note: 1977–2008 wording: In your view, is homosexuality something a person is born with, (or) due to factors such as upbringing and environment?

the Republican Party identifies itself as against abortion and gay marriage then it can draw social conservatives who are less affluent away from the Democratic Party. This will expand the Republican electoral base, reduce the Democratic base and shift the focus of debates to cultural issues and away from economic issues.[22]

As with other issues this scenario, as plausible as it sounds, contains some unknowns and uncertainties. The presumption is that in taking this stance the party only attracts voters and does not alienate any. The difficulty is that those with higher education may be more culturally tolerant and they may dislike the positions of the Republican Party. They may attract lower income voters (though that is by no means clear) but they may also lose other voters.[23] Every position has some costs.

Further, society changes and opinions about some cultural issues shift over time. The issue of gay rights has changed remarkably over time. It was not even a public issue in the 1960s. Over time gay rights advocates started making the case for gay rights. Then groups began to argue that gays should have the same rights to marriage and some states passed laws to that effect. Over time the public has become more accepting of gays.[24] Two trends indicate how a position of a party can become dangerous. Figure 7.3 indicates how opinion about why people are gay has changed over time. In 1978 13 percent thought people were born as gay or lesbian and 56 percent thought it was due to upbringing or environment. Given those opinions, many thought being gay was a choice or due to context and those could be changed. By 2011 the percentage thinking people are born gay increased to 42. Taking a strong stand against gay rights was becoming more risky.

The issue presents a problem for each party. For Democrats, as Table 7.3 indicates, a substantial percentage of those identifying with the party are

Table 7.3 Partisan Opinions on Gay-Related Issues

Legality/Morality of Gay Relations and Views of Origins of Same-Sex Orientation,
by Political Party

	Democrats (%)	Independents (%)	Republicans (%)
People born gay/lesbian	51	41	28
People gay/lesbian due to environment	31	40	55
Gay/lesbian relations should be legal	75	73	41
Gay/lesbian relations should not be legal	23	23	52
Gay/lesbian relations morally acceptable	71	64	30
Gay/lesbian relations morally wrong	26	30	65

Source: Gallup, May 5-8, 2011.

still opposed to gay rights. If the party takes a strong position for such rights, it could cost them some supporters. But opinion is shifting to more tolerant views on the issue. Support for same-sex marriage is steadily increasing, with most of the increase coming among Democrats and Independents.[25]

Republicans also face a dilemma. Among those identifying with the party, a majority holds positions negative about gay rights. Their dilemma is that opinion is shifting to a more accepting position and substantial percentages of their party and of independents are positive about gay rights. While the party has taken positions supporting state referendums to ban gay marriage, continuing with that position could cost the party support in the future. It appears that opinion will continue to become more accepting but how fast change will continue is unknown. The issue presents ambiguities for each party. If Democrats move too fast to support gay rights it could cost the party votes. Continued opposition by Republicans while the society becomes more tolerant of gay rights could cost them votes.

These are just a few examples of the changes that are part of the context of party positioning. Not all issues are like this. In some cases opinions remain relatively stable over time. The percentage of people opposing and supporting abortion rights has been fairly stable.[26] The divisions within the society and the partisan organization of them are fairly clear. In other cases, a consensus that seems to be developing evaporates. At one time many thought that a growing percentage of people were accepting that global warming was occurring and that much of it was man-made. Then the issue became more partisan, some became doubtful that global warming was occurring, and the seeming consensus declined.[27] Now Democrats are faced with the issue of whether to continue to argue for taking action, while Republicans have to worry about looking anti-science if evidence accumulates that global warming is occurring.

Finally, there are changes that emerge and it is not clear whether it will become an issue or not. Each party then has to decide how to react.

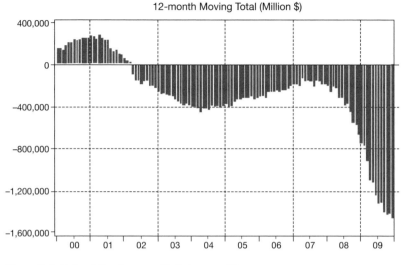

Figure 7.4 Federal Surpluses or Deficits over Time.
Source: U.S. Treasury/Haver Analytics.

The federal government sometimes runs a surplus—taking in more revenue than they spend—but more often runs a deficit. Beginning in 2007, the United States and the world went into recession. Revenues began to decline and deficits reached levels never seen before. Figure 7.4 indicates how much the red ink—symbolizing deficits—began to increase. By 2010 deficits reached $1.5 trillion, which means that the federal government had to borrow that amount each year, increasing the total debt and the amount of federal spending that had to go to repaying the debt and interest to those buying government bonds.

The deficits presented a potential problem but also a potential opportunity for each party. For liberals and most Democrats the conventional answer to the recession and its increasing unemployment and home foreclosures was to employ the logic of Keynesian economics. When the economy slumps the federal government adds to aggregate demand by spending money. In the short-run this boosts spending in the economy and helps the economy grow again, reducing unemployment. The party also thought that they could blame the deficits on President George W. Bush and Republicans, who enacted several large tax cuts during the 2000s and launched two wars without raising taxes to support them. While many were following this logic there was also the concern that with deficits larger than any seen previously the Democrats (who were in control of the presidency and both houses of Congress following the 2008 elections) would be seen as a party engaging in irresponsible economic policies. While most economists embraced the idea of additional government spending, it could not be presumed that the public understood or accepted Keynesian economics.

Republicans faced a difficult choice. Democrats were claiming that Democratic President Bill Clinton had handed George Bush a surplus and the policies of the Republicans had turned that into a deficit. If they opposed spending to help the economy it could also make them look uncaring about unemployment. But the party needed to refurbish its image. Would the public blame Republicans or could the party use the issue as an opportunity to oppose spending and look responsible. The polling data provided contradictory results. Democrats wanted to blame Republicans and some poll results supported that approach.[28] Other polls indicated that an overall majority and a majority within each party blamed excessive spending for the problem.[29] To further confuse matters, other polls indicated that most saw spending for the wars in Iraq and Afghanistan as the problem.[30] Then there was the question of what to do about the deficits. Some polls indicated that a majority wanted to raise taxes on the rich.[31] But the polls just mentioned suggested that there was also support for cutting spending.

The large deficits present an example of a change that many did not anticipate as something that would be a point of serious conflict. The deficits became an issue because they created the need for the federal government to borrow more money. Spending was greater than revenues. The government was following a practice of having Congress approve any increase in the limits of how much total borrowing the government could engage in. Some did not think the vote to borrow more money would be a major issue because in prior years both parties had routinely agreed to increase the debt limit. As will be discussed later, the issue became the basis for a confrontation between the two parties as they sought to position themselves before voters. One side saw them as a serious problem and chose to take a stand.

Events

While long-term changes unfold and present political challenges, abrupt events also occur and a party must decide how to respond. In 2005 Hurricane Katrina struck the Gulf Coast and the Bush administration was presented with how to respond. They faltered and the public developed a negative image of the Bush administration, which in turn hurt the entire party. At the time the hurricane occurred the administration was also incurring criticism about how they were handling the Iraq War. The combination was very detrimental to the reputation of the Bush administration.

Often even what might be a reasonable response to a situation draws negative reactions. In 2009 the Obama administration was presented with the issue of whether to let large banks and the auto industry fail. The argument presented to Obama was that allowing failures would send devastating ripples through the economy and severely damage the entire nation. With some reluctance they finally provided a bailout to both sectors. They argued

Table 7.4 Who's Been Helped by Economic Policies?[a]

| | Total | Party Identification | | |
		Rep	Dem	Indep
Percent who say each has been helped a great deal/fair amount by the federal government's economic policies since 2008				
Wealthy people	57	45	67	58
Middle-class people	27	16	37	28
Small businesses	23	14	35	21
Large corporations	70	61	74	74
Poor people	31	33	33	29
Large banks and financial institutions	74	75	73	77

a Pew Research Center for the People and the Press, "Government Economic Policies Seen as Boon for Banks and Big Business, Not Middle Class or Poor," July 19, 2010: http://pewresearch.org/pubs/1670/large-majorities-say-govt-stimulus-policies-mostly-helped-banks-financial-institutions-not-middle-class-or-poor.

that their efforts had stabilized the economy and prevented a collapse. The hope was that the electorate would give them credit for their efforts. That did not happen. A poll of July of 2010 asked who had benefited from the economic policies of the prior two years (Table 7.4). The results were not comforting. The overwhelming perception was that banks, the wealthy, and large corporations were the primary beneficiaries of economic policies. Even Democrats agreed with this. Democrats had responded to a crisis and thought they would get credit. They did not. How to respond to events that occur abruptly is a major challenge for parties trying to create a positive image within the electorate.

Implications

Political parties are continually faced with social change and the uncertainty of how much an issue will mean to voters. Inequality is continually discussed but few are sure just how many voters will be bothered by it and which argument about how to deal with it will be embraced by a majority. Immigration is an emotional issue but neither party is sure what position to take. Cultural issues flare up but taking strong stands attracts some voters and loses others. Issues such as the deficit emerge and each party has to decide whether this is a temporary issue or one in which they must have a plan to address the issue. Social change never ceases.

8 Voters, Partisanship and the Media

The situation facing parties is fraught with difficulties. They are not certain the long realignment of recent decades has reached stability. Will Republicans gain more of the conservative voters who are now in the Democratic Party? There are differing interpretations of what brought about realignment. Neither has a majority and they must consider who they can attract to achieve a majority and what issues they need to stress to achieve that. While they are positioning themselves, social change can undermine or enhance their strategy. It can thrust new issues on the agenda that most did not anticipate. Forming a party strategy is not simple.

Once a strategy is formed, it must be communicated to voters. That is also not simple. Much of the electorate is disengaged and not paying much attention to the specific positions of parties. The lack of attention creates a need to try to simplify issues and frame how voters see them. Only about one-half of the potential electorate actually votes in a presidential election and in non-presidential elections the rate is even lower. This creates a need to identify likely voters. Then a party must face the issue of how to get their message to likely voters. The process of presentation through "the media" has become more complicated because there are more outlets and fewer people using the traditional outlets. The certainty of getting a message across is less. Finally, with the proliferation of outlets and the growing party polarization, voters have more ability to select the sources they rely on. There is a greater probability that conservatives will choose "conservative" outlets and liberals will choose "liberal" outlets. The message may only get to those who already support the party and not to those the party wants to connect with.

Interest in Politics

Much of the electorate is not very interested in politics (Table 8.1). When asked during a presidential election year whether they are interested in public affairs, only 26.1 percent chose "most of the time" and another 37.5 percent chose "some of the time." When asked about their interest in the upcoming elections, only 43.8 percent chose "very."

Table 8.1 Interest in Politics (2008)

	Hardly at All	Only Now and Then	Some of the Time	Most of the Time
Interest in public affairs?	11.6	24.8	37.5	26.1

	Not Much	Somewhat	Very	
Interest in election	15.5	40.7	43.8	

Source: NES cumulative file, 1948–2008.

The unsurprising result is that surveys regularly indicate that the electorate's knowledge about politics is not high overall but increases with age, education, and interest in politics.[1] Parties operate before an electorate that is not highly attuned to politics. Many people are just not interested and their jobs, families, and other interests consume their attention. Any presentation of party positions must be conducted with the realization that much of the public is not paying attention.

Registering and Voting

The general lack of interest becomes very important when it comes to elections and party strategy. Parties and their candidates seek to win elections. That means paying attention to people who usually register and vote. While many politicians may express their concern for everyone, worrying about those who do not show up at the polls is a chancy and perhaps losing endeavor. There are enduring patterns of who registers and who votes and campaigns are organized with that in mind. Table 8.2 indicates registration and turnout rates in 2008. That is a year of a presidential election, which draws the highest turnout. Even in a year of relatively high interest, there are considerable variations in registration and voting by income and education levels. Those with less education and income are much less likely to register and vote. While party candidates might urge those individuals to vote, the probability is that those with higher incomes and education, and older, will vote more.

The table also indicates the patterns for 1998, known as an off-year election. When there is no presidential contest to stimulate voters their levels of registration and turnout decline. Any party candidate running for election in such a year knows that much of the possible electorate will not vote and the focus must be on those who are likely to vote. Finding out who is likely to vote has become easier in recent years because local boards of election maintain electronic files of registrants. The law now allows a person to stay on the rolls as long as they vote occasionally. To be able to know how frequently someone votes they have to record voting history.

Table 8.2 Registration and Voting by Education and Income, 2008 and 1998 (sum across)

	2008—*Presidential Election*			1998—*Off-Year Election*		
	Not Registered	*Registered, No Vote*	*Registered and Voted*	*Not Registered*	*Registered, No Vote*	*Registered and Voted*
Income Percentile of Population						
0–16	26.4	9.1	64.6	27.7	35.3	36.9
17–33	15.9	10.7	73.5	25.9	30.8	43.3
34–67	11.2	10.3	78.5	18.5	27.8	53.7
68–100	9.5	4.2	86.3	12.8	23.2	64.0
Education						
High school	23.2	11.6	65.2	24.3	33.3	42.5
Some college	8.1	9.6	82.3	20.5	26.2	53.3
College plus	4.5	2.6	92.9	7.4	20.0	72.6

Source: NES Cumulative file, 1948–2008.

That makes it possible to total the number of times an individual has voted in the last six elections and then target those who have a record of voting regularly.

These records also provide an indication of how variations in turnout affect the composition of the voting electorate. Table 8.3 is from a local Board of elections file and indicates how turnout among those registered varies by age. Older people register and vote more than younger people, regardless of the type of election. This shows the distribution of registrants by age, how much each group votes, and the resulting composition of voters. In the presidential year (2008 in this case) 50.5 percent of those between the ages of 18 and 29 voted. While they were 15.7 percent of all registrants, they were only 10.7 percent of voters. Those 60 and over voted at a higher rate and were a larger percentage of voters than of registrants.

When a presidential election does not occur turnout among all groups declines. The right side of Table 8.3 indicates a typical pattern for an off-

Table 8.3 Turnout and the Composition of the Electorate

All Registrants		*Presidential Year*		*Off-Year*	
Age	*% of All*	*Turnout*	*Composition*	*Turnout*	*Composition*
18–29	15.8	50.5	10.7	19.9	6.0
30–44	22.4	67.2	20.3	39.0	16.7
45–59	30.9	81.4	33.9	60.3	35.7
60 plus	31.0	84.1	35.1	70.2	41.6

Note: "% of all" and composition sum down to 100. They indicate the percent of all registrants or actual voters coming from each age group. Turnout indicates the percentage within a group voting.

year election. Turnout is lower for all age groups. The drop, however, is greater for those younger. The result is that the composition of the electorate shifts, with those over 60 constituting a much bigger percent. Those over 60 are 31.0 percent of all registrants but 41.2 percent of voters in this off-year.

These changes in the composition of the electorate can have significant effects on which party wins an election. In 2008 Barack Obama won the presidency and Democrats acquired large majorities in the House and the Senate. Then in 2010 Republicans came close to taking the Senate and did win a majority in the House. There are numerous reasons that might be offered for why Republicans did better. The economy was not generating new jobs and unemployment was relatively high. The enactment of the health care bill in 2010 angered many.[2]

There was also a significant change in who showed up to vote in 2010 versus 2008. In the 2008 elections there were 131,312,072 people who voted in the presidential race. In 2010 the number of people voting for House of Representatives candidates was 86,784,957. There were 44,527,115 fewer voters in 2010 than in 2008. While each party was trying to interpret what the election results meant, one important matter was how the relative composition of the electorate shifted between 2008 and 2010.[3] The differences, drawn from CNN exit polls,[4] can be significant. In 2008 whites were 74 percent of those voting and in 2010 they were 77 percent. Democrats were 40 percent in 2008 and 35 percent in 2010. Republicans were 33 percent in 2008 and 35 percent in 2010. Perhaps most important, conservatives were 34 percent in 2008 and 42 percent in 2010. The composition of the electorate became more favorable to Republicans.

These fluctuations are very important for parties. Republicans might assume that they did so well because of their stance on issues, but they also know that they may have done well because minorities and those with lower incomes are more likely to be Democrats and less likely to vote in an off-year election. The electorate that did not vote in 2010 might show up in 2012. They will change the composition of the electorate and that change could alter who wins the election. For party candidates for congressional seats it means that they must anticipate running in some years in which the electorate has more Democrats and in other years it will have fewer. Presidential candidates may face an electorate consistent in terms of composition, if not mood.

The Role of Partisanship

Parties are continually assessing where they can win votes. Compared to the 1980s, those identifying with either party are now more inclined to vote for the candidate of their party.[5] Figure 8.1 indicates how this changed since 1980 for House candidates. Presidential elections indicate roughly the same pattern of an increase. As discussed in Chapter Four, the parties have

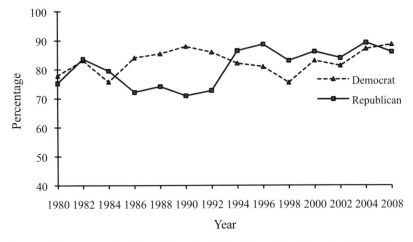

Figure 8.1 Partisan Identifiers Voting for Their House Candidates, 1980–2008.

been experiencing a long-term realignment. Each now has a base that more consistently votes for its candidates. There are still almost 40 percent of voters (depending on the survey) who say they are independent and move back and forth between the two parties. But among those who indicate they identify with a party, loyalty in supporting candidates is increasing. That means that focusing on partisans during a campaign is likely to result in a more certain payoff. Indeed, in the 2004 presidential campaign Karl Rove, political advisor to George Bush, indicated that the strategy was to mobilize the base rather than try to convert anyone.[6]

Partisanship and Likely Voters

These interest and voting patterns endure and become part of the givens of campaigns. Candidates want to devote their resources and attention on those who will respond and vote for them. As they consider the value of spending money to get a message to voters, there is little payoff in sending a message to those likely to vote for the other party. Table 8.4 indicates the partisan situation that parties face.

Those who identify with a party are more likely to say they are very interested in a current election. They pay more attention and follow the issues more than others. They are more likely to register and vote. Those who do not identify with a party have less interest and are less likely to register and vote. Even in a seemingly important presidential election such as 2008 over one-third of independents did not register *and* vote. The consequence is that campaigns face an electorate in which they know that mobilizing partisans will pay off in terms of actually voting and voting for party candidates. These patterns affect party calculations about their positions and who they seek to

Table 8.4 Partisan Identity, Interest and Voting, 2008

	Interest in the Elections			Registration and Voting		
	Not Much	Somewhat	Very	Not Registered	Registered, Did Not Vote	Voted
Republican	6.9	37.3	55.8	5.2	4.4	90.5
Independent	22.9	46.0	31.2	22.5	12.6	64.9
Democrat	12.7	37.0	50.3	9.0	6.8	84.2

Source: NES Cumulative file 1948–2008, for the year 2008.

contact. The enduring challenge is how much to concentrate on mobilizing the base, which is most likely to respond and vote, or to persuading the independents that the other party's policies are bad.

The Changing Media

Assuming a party can determine what their position is and how they are going to present it to voters, the next challenge is to get their message to voters. It is becoming increasingly difficult to widely disseminate a message and assume that it will be received. In the 1950s and 1960s there were essentially three major news outlets—ABC, CBS, and NBC. A considerable percentage of the electorate read a local newspaper or a newsweekly such as *Time, Newsweek,* or *U.S. News and World Report.* If a party wanted to get a message across to voters they would try to get the major television networks and the major news services to report their position and criticism of the other party. If they were successful they had a reasonably good chance of getting their message to those who were somewhat attentive to news. Those uninterested would miss it, but much of the attentive public would get the message.

Since then the nature of mass media has changed considerably.[7] The number of cable television channels has exploded with almost all of them devoted to entertainment. Consumers have much more choice and many of them are choosing not to watch the national evening news shows. Those uninterested in politics can specifically avoid having to watch any political shows. The percentage of the public watching presidential debates has declined. Newspaper readership has also declined, and as this has occurred newspapers have less revenue from advertising to hire reporters to cover politics. The result is newspapers with less news and fewer readers. Party members cannot assume that if they form and present a message that it will reach a substantial percentage of possible voters. It is now quite possible for a national issue to consume politicians in Washington for a week or two and encounter people who have no idea a controversy has emerged. They are simply accessing other media outlets and not interested or aware.

While traditional news sources are being utilized less, cable shows and the internet are becoming a growing source of information for many.[8] Their rise presents an opportunity and a problem for political parties. These newer sources provide more opportunities for individuals to select their sources of information and many people are selecting them because they see them as sources compatible with their views. Conservatives trust some sources more than others and liberals trust other sources.[9] Voters can now select, particularly on the internet, the presentation and interpretation of news. The opportunity for the parties is to rely on these sources to present their case and seek to motivate their base to contribute, work for the party, and donate resources. They can regularly appear on particular channels and commentary shows to make their case as to how things should be seen. The opportunity is to effectively target the message to a specific audience that is interested.

The difficulty, however, is that getting a message to a wider audience becomes harder. No single outlet in America has such a wide audience that it can be presumed that a message will get through. This, combined with the disinterest of many, means that a party may have devoted considerable energy to presenting a position on a current issue, yet a poll can indicate that many Americans have paid no attention to the issue.

Implications

The varying interest levels of the public and the changing media have had several effects on parties. They have created behaviors that trouble much of the public, but that parties see as a necessary response to this situation.

First, parties realize that getting a message through to largely uninterested and uninformed voters is difficult. Their attention span is short and many will see a message only once. As a result, they devote considerable attention to simplification and framing. They will prepare background papers, hold lengthy hearings, and develop detailed critiques of the proposals of the other party, but few voters will ever be aware of that information. They also have to focus on a message that will be short and will get on the news. If possible, it has to constitute a good "sound-bite," or a statement short enough that it will make it on-air or will be prominent in a written story. The goal is to get the frame before the public.

President Ronald Reagan was successful in getting attention for his statement "Government is not the solution, government is the problem." His message that he did not believe another government program was the solution to social problems came through. President Bill Clinton sought to convey his position that there should be limits to benefits from programs with the message "a hand up, not a hand out." When Republicans submitted legislation to limit the availability of welfare they entitled the bill "The Personal Responsibility and Work Opportunity Act." When

Democrats were seeking to enact the Affordable Care Act in 2010 to expand access to health care they consistently told stories about individuals faced with serious health care problems. The goal was to convey the message that the legislation would help those in need. Republicans countered with references to big government choosing your doctor and the loss of individual freedom. In all such cases the emphasis is on simple messages and endless repetition. The goal of a party official is to "stay on message." This means adopting a message and repeating it in multiple settings.

The battle in 2012 over whether contraception should be a required benefit for women in health insurance programs is an important example of how complexity is displaced by competing frames as the parties seek to establish positions and connect with voters. The health care legislation passed in 2010 set standards for what health insurance benefits had to be provided. The issue of contraception presented a delicate problem. The Catholic Church opposes birth control and a requirement to provide it would conflict with their views. Yet to not provide it would mean women employees would have to pay for birth control separately. President Obama sought to finesse the issue by saying the church would not have to pay for and provide birth control but the regulations would require that insurance companies provide it as part of their packages. The issue quickly became the Republican criticism of a Democratic president infringing on religious freedom and government intrusion versus the Democratic concern about women's health care needs rights. Each party was playing to its base and simplifying the issue into sound bites and each thought they would fare well with their framing.[10]

What was lost in the framing of the issue was the complexity of the role of Catholic hospitals. The Catholic Church owns and runs many hospitals and as the merger of hospitals in the nation occurs they are acquiring others.[11] While the issue was discussed in 2012, the issue of how many religiously run hospitals there are and what policies should apply to what is not an exercise in religion but a medical and business activity and its employees were completely lost. The complex issue of how religion and business mesh was lost and voters were presented with two simple and competing ways to think about the issue.

This annoys many voters to no end. Many voters feel like they are being presented with simplistic responses to complicated situations. Politicians appear on news shows and repeat the same simple messages again and again. The United States' debt is rising steadily and each party offers robotic messages of "maintaining programs that people need" (Democrats) versus "facing up to the limits of what we can do" (Republicans). One stresses the needs and the other stresses fiscal limits. While many are annoyed, each party is sending its essential message to an electorate that knows little detail of the situation. Few know what current tax rates are, how many people benefit from programs, and what alternative proposals exist for responding to the rising costs of government programs. To those who follow politics closely, these responses are inadequate and frustrating. To those who do not follow politics much and may vote, these messages convey basic stances. This simplification is a reasonable response to an electorate that is only somewhat engaged.

The situation of many voters with limited interest and media outlets that do not provide regular explanations of the policy disagreements between the parties prompts party candidates to find another way to get their message to voters. Their means is the commercial, with television increasingly the medium. If newspapers are not going to detail the policy positions of their opponents, the best way to get that information to voters is through television ads. If ads are going to be effective they have to get the attention of voters. The best way to do that is have ads that make some emotional connection, that present evidence that your opponent has betrayed some fundamental value of Americans. Your opponent does not care about life (is pro-abortion rights) or does not respect the rights of women (is anti-abortion rights). Your opponent does not care about the security of America (voted against the PATRIOT Act passed following 9/11) or is in favor of trampling on the rights of Americans (voted for the PATRIOT Act). Your opponent does not care about the future of our children (voted for a budget with large deficits, requiring more government debt) or does not care about those vulnerable (voted to cut the budget and social programs). The simpler and the more tied to a fundamental and emotional value the better. Those ads present clear messages and if well done get the attentions of those sitting at home. Many voters do not like this barrage of ads and their negative tone, but if a party is going to get its message across to those less engaged, it needs ads with a clear simple message.

Then there comes the matter of acquiring the resources to pay for all these ads. Politicians need money to produce and air ads and they need to repeat these ads as many times on as many shows as they can. Given the fragmentation of the media, it is not enough to put ads on the major networks. They need to be on a variety of cable shows at all times of the day to get to specific audiences. This takes money. Television stations in America are not required to offer any free air time to campaigns and, to their delight, they are able to charge the highest rates for political ads. Campaigns want lots of repetition and that requires lots of money.

All this puts parties and their candidates in a difficult situation. They need money. They also know that there is considerable concern in America about the growing role of money. The affluent and interest groups have much more capability to contribute. Party candidates know that several Supreme Court decisions have made it easier for the affluent to raise money for campaigns.[12] The reality for parties is that they have no alternative but to solicit and accept money from those who have it to offer. For Republicans this has been an easier situation because they argue that the successful should be respected and seen as the ones who generate jobs and tax revenue in

America. They want to avoid appearing to be beholden to the most affluent, but accepting their money is not a fundamental conflict for the party. For Democrats, seeking contributions from the most affluent has been a greater source of unease, but they also need money to conduct campaigns. Democrats are in the situation of bemoaning the role of money in politics in general, and particularly the role of money coming from Wall Street, but they still need money. At the same time many within the party are expressing their concern about inequality in America and the growth in CEO compensation. Yet, because they need money for campaigns the party and its candidates are just as aggressive as Republicans in seeking money from those who have it.

The result is that parties appear to be hypocritical. They speak of the people but they continually solicit money to run their campaigns from those with high incomes. It makes many voters cynical about who is dominating representation in Washington. Party candidates understand that and may wish it was otherwise, but, again, with many of the public only somewhat interested and a fragmented media, they need lots of money to present and repeat their message. They also need to have lots of money available in case a credible set of ads are run against them during a campaign and they need to run counter ads in a hurry. That possibility makes them even more inclined to raise money.

That does not mean that a party gives up on its principles. But it does make them realize that if they take money from interest groups they need to make sure they let them in turn make their case to a Member of Congress who is elected using the interest group's money. They usually feel the obligation to listen. They may temper the tone of their criticism of the stance of a group that contributed to the party. They need money to present their case to voters, but they know they cannot look too cozy and responsive to contributors. Both parties may be more responsive to the affluent than would occur without our current campaign finance system.[13] It is a challenge for parties to handle well.

Finally, the variations in who votes also affect the positions of parties. Anyone who campaigns knows that those older vote more than anyone else and younger people vote at lower rates, even in presidential elections. It should be no surprise that both parties recognize the problem of the growing cost of programs such as Medicare (which covers the health care costs of those 65 and older) but both are very careful how they talk about constraining the program. Democrats and Republicans realize some constraints are necessary but do not want seniors to see them as hurting the program. The result is the critics of the program's costs always present their proposals as intended to "save" the program in the future. In 2010 Democrats enacted "reforms" in Medicare, which would save billions of dollars over time and said they only involved eliminating "waste." They did not want to suggest they were curtailing the program. Republicans, who have been more inclined to want to restrain growth in the program, focus on saving the program and empowering individuals to make their own choices about who provides their coverage. Both want to avoid a clear impression that they are curtailing Medicare, a position that would antagonize those over 65. Who votes affects the focus of public policy debates.

9 Enduring Uncertainty and Troubling Behaviors

We continually seek to understand the broad factors shaping political divisions in America. Academics, consultants, and commentators review data and try to discern what explains trends. While many valuable studies interpret how we got to where we are, party strategists must decide what to do for upcoming elections. As they do so they face continual uncertainty. They need to review and consider what happened in the past, but their primary focus has to be what is shaping conditions now and what will matter in the future.

There are a myriad of factors that create considerable uncertainty about that. There has been a long-term realignment, but it is unclear whether it will continue. Should they accept the current differences in bases between the parties or can they emphasize some positions and attract more voters from the other party. They have to decide what brought them voters and whether the same factors are relevant now. If they do decide to emphasize a theme, will it cost them more voters than it attracts. If Democrats focus on inequality issues, will that drive away middle-class voters who see themselves as paying for social programs? If Republicans choose to focus on cultural issues will it cost them more of the more educated and tolerant?

They make these decisions knowing that neither has a majority within the electorate or across congressional districts. A wrong emphasis could cost them that 10 percent in the middle who can swing to or away from a party and cost them an election. The lack of a majority means that they may have to let some candidates separate themselves from the party to establish more of an independent image. If they elect Members in swing districts they may have to decide whether to ask those Members to vote with the party.

They also have to try to anticipate social change and how it will be seen by the public. There are broad trends such as the rise of non-whites in American society and the increase in inequality. Should Republicans take a stand against more immigration even as it continues and it becomes difficult to remove illegal immigrants? Someday they will become a significant political bloc and that bloc could vote against them. Should Democrats make inequality a theme or will this just make them look like they are in favor of redistribution and envy the successful? There are also short-term factors to try and anticipate. Will the economy improve or decline? If a party bets it will decline and they attack and it improves how will the party look on election day?

Finally, even if they can sort all this out, there is the challenge of whether their way of presenting an issue will connect with voters. Many voters pay no attention and the party may struggle to get their message through the fragmented media. The uncertainties that parties face are endless. They require relentless assessments of how issues are playing, how voter sentiment is evolving, and how the strategy of the party is working. We now turn to a more detailed review of how these matters play out.

This uncertainty creates behaviors that many voters do not like. A party makes a position in favor of a particular policy proposal and then alters their commitment as they sense that the reaction to it among swing voters is negative. Or they promise passage of a bill when they acquire a majority and never pass it because the members in marginal districts become worried how the vote will look. Republicans stress cultural issues because their strategists tell them that these positions did attract voters and will win over more, but subsequent polls indicate that they are alienating more than they are attracting. The focus on cultural issues then diminishes, disappointing those who took the party to be sincere. Democrats state that they favor "a path to citizenship" for immigrants who have paid taxes and have good work records, but the eruption of the Tea Party sends a signal that their stance is angering and motivating these voters to vote and vote against Democrats. Some segments of the Republican Party speak passionately about the importance of limiting gay rights, but others read the trends in polls toward acceptance of gays and try to get the party to back off such rhetoric. These behaviors stem from each party struggling with understanding what got them the electoral support they have, with recognition that neither has a majority, and with unease about how to react to social trends. It is not that the parties lack principles, but reading the political environment is not a simple process. Parties stake out a position, and may well fully believe in it, but if poll results suggest that continuing with that position will hurt in the upcoming elections, they adjust.

Parties also simplify issues enormously. Voters are subjected to sound bites and slogans. Politicians appear on television and stay on message and avoid answering questions with any specifics. They do so because they are trying to get a message across to voters who are in general only somewhat engaged. While they appear to be robots, they are trying to keep their message clear and simple with the hopes that their framing of the issue will appear in headlines and news stories in subsequent days. Those voters who have some awareness of the issues become annoyed, but for many others the simplified message is all they will ever hear. The behavior of parties, troubling as it may be to many voters, is largely driven by how they see the political context within which they work. Their behavior may annoy voters, but it is a rational adaptation to reality.

Part III

Pursuing Party Goals

10 Pursuing Coalitions and an Identity
Long-Term Strategies

Political parties are one of our primary vehicles for representing public concerns. Members of a party have views about how society should work, about the role government should play, and about the policies that should be adopted. In a democratic society the ideal is that parties seek to organize and represent a coalition that reflects these ideas. They organize voters with different ideas, select candidates who articulate these ideas, present themselves to the electorate, and act on their principles if they win elections. To many voters that ideal is not fulfilled. Parties present platforms and many voters doubt that they follow through. Members often seem more preoccupied with specific events and castigating the behavior of the other party than with presenting coherent policies and acting on them. They seem preoccupied with posturing when voters want action.

The previous chapters detailed some of the difficulties that parties face in presenting themselves to voters. The conditions create continual uncertainty about how parties should position themselves. While the examples focus on relatively recent situations, uncertainty has been a constant for political parties. This uncertainty has been particularly relevant because each party has undergone considerable change over time. Each party has sought to create a coalition reflecting its core concerns, even as society and the issues of the day have changed. All of the conditions just reviewed make reading the political context difficult. It leads to behaviors that trouble voters but are part of parties trying to attract new voters by presenting issue positions and then often pulling back when they cannot muster the votes to take action or sense a proposal is not being received well as details emerge. Building a coalition is an endlessly challenging endeavor in a political world where many voters do not pay attention, the media does not cover matters well, and how voters will react is unknown. The next two chapters are an effort to explain how this works over the long run and the short run.

Parties are engaged in two processes at any one time. They are engaged in a long-run strategy to build a majority coalition.[1] That means identifying a majority that reflects their basic beliefs and consistently pursuing actions to attract them. While parties have long-term plans, they also are continually monitoring the political environment for short-term situations that will provide them with an opportunity to send a message to voters about their values and their competencies and the deficiencies in the other party. That means devoting considerable energy to trying to exploit immediate situations to enhance their image and diminish the image of their opponents.

To simplify the presentation, this chapter deals with long-term strategies and the next chapter deals with responses to short-term conditions. This separation of the long-term and short-term strategies of parties is artificial. For the most part a party sees the effort to exploit a short-term issue as just another way to establish their policy image and indicate what government should be doing. If government funded unemployment compensation benefits are expiring and a Democrat is president then Republicans may see this as an opportunity to expound on individual responsibility to find jobs, on the need to limit government spending, and to note the failures of the president to generate jobs. Democrats may see this as an opportunity to present themselves as caring for those unemployed. In these situations, separating long-term and short-term strategies is difficult. A decision juncture is exploited to reinforce a long-term party image but also present the other party as not handling an immediate situation well.

Other times unexpected events occur and do not fit well into a long-term strategy but they provide a chance to portray the other party as incompetent. When Hurricane Katrina occurred in August 2005 and the response was badly handled by the Bush administration it became an opportunity for Democrats to bash a Republican president as incompetent. When a British Petroleum oil rig in the Gulf of Mexico sprang a leak and poured millions of gallons of oil into the Gulf, Republicans in Congress sought to portray the Democratic administration of Barack Obama as incompetent in its response. We will turn to these short-term matters in the next chapter.

Forming a Party Identity and Creating a Coalition

We start with the long-term challenges parties face. They want a majority coalition. They may be in the minority and they need to attract voters who do not have a history of voting for them. Given this situation, why do parties indicate they may enact a policy and then fail to do so or enact something considerably less than what they promised. Why do they indicate sympathy for a group and then not act on that sympathy? Why do they indicate they want a policy and then pull back on it? Much of the public sees this as deception. It appears that a policy was proposed to win office rather than office was won to enact a policy.

Parties are not without fundamental principles. Republicans believe in individualism, the value of capitalism, limited government, and their sense that traditional norms should be followed. Democrats believe many individuals do not have opportunity and should, that concentrations of economic power are dangerous, that government can play a role in redressing inequities, and that there should be tolerance for diverse ways of living. Over time each party wants to attract those who believe in their views. That means sending signals to voters who they think will support them. While that process sounds simple, as political change occurs the party may have a substantial part of their base that opposes pursuing a new base or enacting new ideas. This leads to what the public often sees as behavior they regard as inconsistent, insincere, or erratic.

The reason for inconsistent party behavior is that when a party proposes different policies to alter or expand its electoral base it encounters two problems. Voters do not change their party identification quickly.[2] The proposal may not attract enough of the voters that a party sought to attract and leave the party wondering whether the proposal is going to win the group over. It may also find that the new policies are not embraced by the older base. When it comes to enactment, Members of Congress from the older base resist and decline to go along with the proposals. Indeed, they may return to enacting policies that reflect the older base and risk alienating the potential new voters. The policy proposals may have sounded good for the purposes of a campaign, but the older base may represent a constituency that has disagreements with the proposed policies. Representatives of the older base need considerable convincing before they will go along. That results in the appearance of insincere policy proposals. A proposal is presented but, assuming a majority is won, it may not be pushed once in power. This process has played out over time because each party at some time in recent decades has faced the situation of being in the minority and the need to expand and even fundamentally change its coalition. The combination of voters who do not change their party loyalty easily and Members from the old base may lead a party to present a policy proposal but abandon it or not be able to convince the old base to go along.

Eras of Minority Status

The need to attract voters and make new policy proposals stems from a party being in the minority. If a party is a minority for a sustained time period, they have to think how to attract new voters. That leads to new policies, internal conflicts between an old and a potential base, and what many voters see as insincere or erratic policy positions. There have been distinct time periods when one of the major parties in America was in the minority. No party wishes to stay in that status and it drives a party to focus on how to attract a broader constituency. The broad outlines of these eras are shown in Table 10.1. Presidential results are used because they provide a rough guideline of what was happening in presidential and congressional elections.[3]

From 1900 to 1928 Republicans dominated American politics, winning six of eight presidential elections. Then from 1932 to 1964 Democrats dominated, winning the presidential contest in seven out of nine elections.

Table 10.1 Party Success in Presidential Elections by Years, 1900–2004

Years	Party and Campaigns Won	Democratic % of		Republican % of	
		Popular Vote	Electoral College	Popular Vote	Electoral College
1900–1928	R—6/8	40.1	39.3	50.2	60.7
1932–1964	D—7/9	52.6	66.0	45.8	34.0
1968–2004	R—7/10	44.9	36.5	49.3	63.5

Note: The percentages shown are averages of the national percentages for the years indicated. The elections included stop with 2004 because the focus is on how past results shape candidate calculations. The 2008 results are not included because they will affect the 2012 calculations, an election outside the scope of this analysis.

Then from 1968 to 2004 Republicans won seven of ten elections. In each of these eras the minority party was faced with the need to find a way to attract more voters. In each era the minority party struggled with presenting a consistent policy image to voters because of the tensions between the old and potentially new part of their coalition. In each era the minority party often appeared conflicted and inconsistent to voters. The goal in what follows is not a comprehensive review of this history, but brief summaries of how the challenge of creating a long-term change in a coalition can create some inconsistencies of behavior.

Democrats 1900–1928

From 1900 through 1928 the Democratic Party was in the minority. Their base was the South and it was inadequate to get the party close to a majority. Fifty percent of the population and Electoral College votes were in the North. The party knew they had to attract voters in northern areas, and they thought their best bet was to focus on urban workers with a message that the party would work to improve their working conditions. The party sponsored legislation to support labor and tax the affluent to convey their support for urban workers.[4] The consistency of the party's message to that urban constituency always faltered and became murky because the potential base conflicted with the traditional base. The South was not friendly to Catholics and immigrants and the northern cities were filled with these people. The result was that the party said it was trying to help urban voters but its image was still rural, agricultural and inhospitable to Catholic immigrants.[5]

While the party was telling northern urban immigrants that it supported them, Democrats were also voting for prohibition and for strict limits on further immigration. Any voter seeking to sort out just what the party stood for would probably have been confused about the party's message as the existing and possible bases of the party battled over what policies it should endorse. The party may have been sincere in its claims of concern for urban workers, but its expression of that concern was erratic as the older and newer bases struggled to influence party positions.

Republicans 1932–1964

Following the Great Depression the electorate rejected Republicans and gave Democrat Franklin Roosevelt the presidency and his party a substantial majority in Congress. There was a fundamental shift in which party the electorate supported. This left Republicans largely in the minority for the next 30 years. The party lost the presidency in seven of nine elections. They usually were in the minority in Congress. The result was that gradually a conflict developed within the party about how to get out of their minority status. There were those who thought that the national programs that Democrats enacted in the 1930s—Social Security, welfare, unemployment compensation, regulations favoring unions—should be accepted and the party had to be moderate. There was another faction that strongly believed that the party had to provide a conservative alternative to Democrats or there would be no reason for anyone to vote Republican. The result was a divided party.[6] Eventually, conservatives mounted a strong effort to assert themselves and nominate more conservative candidates. In 1964 they succeeded by nominating for president the true conservative Barry Goldwater.[7]

While he was beaten badly, that race was the beginning of a battle within the Republican Party over how conservative the party should be.[8] The party was being advised that the South was more conservative and that the best bet for the party was to pursue a Southern Strategy of appealing to conservatives.[9] It was also the beginning of a time when Republicans presented a mixed and sometimes confusing image to voters. Republican Richard Nixon campaigned as the party's nominee in 1968 and won. His administration was conflicted about how to appeal to the South and how much to try to retain its older base in the North. Civil rights issues were especially difficult for the party. Nixon knew that the North had been reliably Republican for decades and a candidate never walks away from voters inclined to support him. Yet he knew the party needed to expand into the South. The North was not sympathetic to the segregation and denial of rights occurring in the South so he could not make his appeal too accommodating. As a result, he regularly indicated he would support civil rights legislation, but only as the law required. He also spoke of states' rights, which was taken as code language for he would not push enforcement too much. The result was continual ambiguity as to where he stood.[10] His goal was to retain the older base because there was uncertainty about how much he could attract the newer base. The South had been Democratic for a century and he had to be careful how he balanced northern and southern concerns. The result was the appearance of inconsistent and insincere policy proposals. Nixon was trying to appeal to both regions of the country while trying to win over the South. He sent mixed signals out of necessity.

Republicans: The 1970s and after

The 1960s were a significant juncture in American politics. Both parties were beginning the process of seeking changes in their electoral bases. Republicans had been frustrated by their lengthy minority status and were trying to get out of that situation. They were making an appeal to the South to try to win votes there. While the party was becoming more committed to the idea of pursuing the South, the issue of what was driving change became a major issue.[11] Some argued that Republicans were capitalizing on racial resentments to win over white southerners. If that was the case the party should continue to speak in language related to race. There was also evidence that Republicans were gaining because they were attracting business and the more affluent. The argument was that class divisions were driving change.[12] Others suggested that cultural issues were more important. The South holds more fundamentalists and appealing to them about race, abortion, gay rights, and crime appeared to be working.

The issue of just what was driving change, discussed in Chapter Five, was a very real issue for Republicans. Should they vaguely discuss race? Or should the focus be on issues of the rising costs of entitlement programs, tax cuts for the affluent, and opposition to redistribution as a way to win the middle class and above. Or should they focus on cultural issues such as abortion and opposition to gay rights and same-sex marriage. Which of these were most important to voters the party was trying to attract? These decisions involve not just who might be attracted, but who might be lost. Vague references to race will drive away those who think it is dangerously divisive or who worry that there is some discrimination in America and we need to address it. Focusing on program cuts and opposition to redistribution will alienate some who think there is some merit to these programs. Focusing on abortion and gays will lose those who support tolerance and do not want government involved in these matters. Emphasizing one theme will win some and lose some others.

The result has been a party that has vacillated in its focus. A major focus of the party since Ronald Reagan was restraining the growth of government. During the 1990s Republicans in the House presented the Contract with America that advocated for significant cuts in government programs. After winning the House in the 1994 elections, Speaker Newt Gingrich threatened to shut down government unless the Republican budget cuts were accepted by President Bill Clinton. Despite the convictions of many Republicans that this was a good maneuver, public opinion turned against them and Republicans eventually capitulated. In the 2000s, with the federal government having a surplus of revenues, President George W. Bush and the Republicans pushed through a major tax cut. They did not cut programs by equivalent amounts. The country also engaged in wars in Afghanistan and Iraq and enacted an expensive prescription drug program for seniors. Then budget deficits began to grow and there was consistent criticism within the party that they had lost their identity as the party of fiscal responsibility.

Parties try to respond to shape voter perceptions. After George W. Bush left the presidency and Barack Obama became president, the party decided to re-emphasize its commitment to fiscal responsibility. With the economy losing jobs rapidly in 2009 President Obama proposed a stimulus bill— a combination of tax cuts and spending to get the economy going. Republicans decided to oppose the package to present the party as more fiscally responsible. When Democrats proposed the Affordable Care Act to expand health care coverage the party uniformly opposed it as fiscally irresponsible and not the responsibility of government. During the summer of 2011 the party refused to pass an increase in the debt limit, or the amount of money the federal government can borrow, arguing that deficits were too large and government spending needed to be cut. The goal, at a time when the federal deficit has been over $1 trillion dollars and debt is increasing, has been to establish the primary and consistent image of the Republican Party as the fiscally responsible party. Many felt that they lost that focus during the time when George W. Bush was president and they needed to re-establish that as their primary concern.

But the party also knew that some of its success was due to the ability to attract social conservatives. As they attracted more of these voters there were desires and pressures to focus more on related issues. Despite the party's efforts to define the party with a focus on fiscal issues, there are occasional events that distract them from that focus. Legislation is considered that involves an issue crucial to the social conservative wing of the party. The members committed to this concern are passionate about the issue and seek to use the opportunity to affect policy. The media is attracted to the controversy and gives it considerable attention. That muddies the effort to define the fiscal focus of the party.

During the 1980s and 1990s, Republicans were attracting social conservatives and party members sounded as if they would respond to them. But the party was uneasy about looking intolerant. Republicans in the early 2000s were willing to pass legislation in Congress to limit partial-birth abortions. Some members of the party were willing to try to ban abortion completely, but there was unease among others within the party about trying to eliminate a woman's right to make the choice of whether to have an abortion.

In the 2004 presidential election, Karl Rove, President Bush's chief political advisor, was convinced the party needed some way to mobilize social conservatives to vote in specific states. As a means to energize them he worked with state officials to get referenda on state ballots affirming marriage was only between a man and a woman. The hope was that this would draw more social conservatives to the polls. While it may have, it reinforced the image that the party was preoccupied with morality issues.

As a party responds to a part of its coalition they often misjudge how their actions will be received. They can go too far in their effort to send a message to a particular constituency. By the mid 2000s Republicans had been seeking support among social conservatives for at least two decades. There was, however, grumbling among some social conservatives that the party had not really delivered. In 2005 an opportunity emerged for the party to indicate its support for "the culture of life." A woman named Terri Schiavo had been on life support for several years and had no recorded brain activity. Her husband wanted to remove the feeding tube that kept her alive. Her parents did not want it removed, but her husband had the legal right to make that decision. The case went to court and the court decided the husband could authorize removing the feeding tube. Republicans in Congress saw this as an example of courts intruding on issues in a way that did not respect the sanctity of life. They controlled both houses of Congress and passed legislation to override the court decision. President Bush flew back from his ranch in Crawford, Texas at midnight to sign the legislation. It was a high profile effort to establish an identity.

The difficulty was that the public thought it was an inappropriate intrusion into decisions that should be made by families. Polls indicated that 76 percent of all Americans thought it was inappropriate for Congress to become involved. Even those who thought it was wrong to remove the feeding tube disapproved. Among Republicans, 65 percent disapproved. Most people thought this should be a family decision.[13] It was a case where appealing to a base the party wanted to attract was not well received.

The desire for action on social issues persists within the Republican Party. During the passage of the Affordable Health Care Act of 2010 some Members of the party were sure that the legislation would allow for government funding of abortion. They sought to hold up the legislation and insert more clauses banning any such possibility. In 2012 several state legislatures controlled by Republicans sought to influence abortions by requiring that a woman have an ultrasound procedure prior to the abortion by having an ultrasound rod inserted into their vagina. They would also have to have the image described to them by a doctor. While some within the party were trying to emphasize economic issues, the social conservative wing of the party was committed to legislation they saw as representing moral concerns. The social conservatives within the party believe in these efforts and want more emphasis on morality issues. The result is that the party focuses on cultural issues and then pulls back. Many social conservatives within the party see considerable inconsistency and perhaps insincerity in the positions taken by Republicans.

To return to earlier concerns, this process of image creation is a challenge and a gamble because of the conditions they face. They face an electorate that does not pay a great deal of attention. The media often does not cover the concerns the party has and often treats the positions taken as a game, a false posture to look like they stand for something.[14] Republicans think that most Americans are conservative but they are not sure they really are. They have to presume that swing voters are primarily concerned with program cuts and that these voters will accept the argument that spending cuts will lead to job growth. They need to simplify their stance—limit the growth of government spending—and repeat it as much as possible because most voters are only paying limited attention.

No party is unified and various groups within the party may have strong beliefs about what issues should be pursued. While the party may wish to define itself with one consistent emphasis it cannot deny those who wish to emphasize other issues because of their beliefs. Republicans have devoted sustained efforts since the 1980s to attract those with strong religious and moral values to the party. That has brought the party some strong supporters. They cannot very well stifle them and retain their support. The result is some ambiguity in the image presented to voters about the fundamental concerns of the party. Is it concerned with the economy and jobs or with establishing moral codes? As long as there is no clear majority with a single concern to represent, parties face this problem of inconsistency of image.

Democrats: The 1970s and after

The Democratic Party has had its own issues about how to position itself and the resulting inconsistencies. Just as with the Republicans they have struggled with interpreting what is creating change and how they should respond. In contrast with Republicans, who were trying to gain supporters, Democrats were trying to determine why they lost supporters. In the 1950s and 1960s considerably more people identified as Democratic than Republican. Then their support began to erode and the issue of what shapes party loyalties became very important. The party was bombarded with interpretations and what it should do. As reviewed in Chapter Five, the party was presented with arguments that it had shown too much sympathy for Blacks and was losing whites, or that it had become too much of a collection of cultural liberals with elites too concerned with gay rights, abortion, and environmental issues. It had to decide several matters. Could it afford to lose the South and survive? If not, should they show less concern for race issues such as affirmative action? Were they not showing enough concern for working class whites?[15] Should they try to de-emphasize cultural issues? Should they stay away from or embrace immigration and more respect for immigrants? Were non-whites growing fast enough as a percentage of the electorate (and were they registering) to provide a replacement of the whites they were losing?

For the most part the dominant view within the party was that they had to present a less liberal image to the electorate and it had to focus more on providing opportunity while expecting responsibility and initiative from those receiving benefits. They needed to indicate greater concern for the economic problems of the middle class. They also had to reduce the sense that the party was hostile to business.[16] The challenge was to find issues that would communicate these concerns to voters and establish the party as sympathetic to minorities but not as beholden to them. They responded to initiatives from Republicans and also developed their own themes. When President Ronald Reagan sought to reform the income tax laws to reduce various loopholes and make them fairer, Democrats went along. They did not want to look opposed to a fair tax system. Republicans won the House in 1994 and wanted to limit welfare usage to five years during a lifetime and two years at any one time. Democrats went along because they did not want appear to support a program providing unlimited benefits. Democrats supported greater grants for students to attend college. They pushed for an expanded Earned Income Tax Credit (EITC) which provides for a tax refund if a person is working and their income falls below a certain amount. The idea was to convey their support for those with low incomes if they were working. The party supported job training programs and higher taxes on the more affluent. Their goal was to stress programs that helped those who worked (EITC) or were trying to improve themselves (job training and college).

Just as with the Republicans, however, the "cultural wars" were a dilemma. Was it the case that the party was increasingly attracting social liberals and should they continue to stress abortion and gay rights, and advocate for policies to counter global warming? Was it the case that the working class was really opposed to all these matters and would this contradict their economic message? Just as with the Republicans there was a wing of the party that cared deeply about these issues and those Members were not willing to be quiet at various times. When Republicans sought to limit abortion and ban same-sex marriage Democrats were prominent opponents. When Republicans asserted there was no proof of global warming and that it was a hoax Democrats opposed them. The party was continually worried that they were seen as the party of cultural liberals with an uneasy connection to traditional morals. The cultural issues often pulled them away from economic issues and created some doubt about which of the two was of a higher priority.

These tensions over image emerged during the Obama administration. He was presented with issues of "don't ask and don't tell." This involves the issue of whether the military will avoid issues of whether gays can serve in the military. The existing policy was to allow gays to serve in the military as long as no one announces they are gay. After some delay he and the Democrats were able to pass legislation to ban discrimination against gays in the military. There was also the issue of whether Obama would support an effort to make same-sex marriages legal nationally by advocating for legislation in Congress. Despite having said he favored gay marriage he advocated for civil unions until he announced his support for it in 2012. Overall, the Obama administration engaged in a delicate balancing act, trying not to let these issues define the party, but showing support for those gays who had voted for the party in 2008.[17]

The pattern has been one of some hesitancy and vacillation, for two reasons. First, for the last two decades the party has been presented with regular arguments that it has become too closely identified with liberal cultural positions that are favored more by elites than by the general public. The advice has been to tone down the attention drawn to these issues or risk losing the votes of those with less education or who adhere to more traditional values. Second, despite all the discussion about the parties becoming more homogeneous, there are still many Members in Congress within the Democratic Party who represent constituencies not favorable to gays. They might like to go along, but think it would be detrimental to their re-election prospects. The ongoing argument that the party should de-emphasize liberal cultural positions plus some party members who are reluctant to vote for liberal policies results in party hesitation to act. As the party was struggling with these issues, many saw the pattern as a case of politicians who promise something but then will not deliver when in office.[18]

Issues of party diversity emerged during the enactment of the Affordable Health Care Act. Democrats originally proposed a "public option" which meant that government would provide a government managed alternative to compete with private business. The goal was to restrain the growth of premiums by having competition. As the process continued, opponents settled on the slogan of an ominous "government takeover" of health care. Democrats in Congress worried about the image and the effects on private companies and withdrew their support. A policy that was proposed was withdrawn and many saw the Democrats as having misrepresented their intentions. The difficulty was a lack of support within the party.

All of the issues discussed in chapters four through eight are relevant as parties struggle to present a set of policy positions to create an image and a majority coalition. There has been considerable change in which regions of the nation and which social groups support each party. They are uncertain precisely how much some issues have brought them voters and cost them others. They are presented with numerous interpretations and can never be sure which ones are really valid. In an age of around-the-clock news coverage, internet essayists, and more and more political consulting firms, there is a wide array of interpretations presented to them. Both parties know they do not have a stable majority and that ongoing social change makes it possible that what was a near majority could erode in the near future. They want to present their case to voters in some detail, but know that most of the position-taking and legislative proposals in Washington will not be known to most voters and what is presented may be enormously simplified by the media and distorted by opponents.

The pursuit of a majority is an iterative process. Members of a party have basic beliefs, but they are unsure how much to stress them at any one time. They try one emphasis and gauge the way it is received. They watch how the criticism of their opponents is received and adjust based on their assessment of that. They also have to deal with the diversity within their party and their views of what the party should do.

The result is a series of presentations that greatly trouble voters. There are changes in policy proposals that are meant to indicate responsiveness but some see as reneging on a campaign promise. There are simplifications of an issue to get a message to voters through the media. To some this is distortion. These are a result of a party engaged in adjustments as they gauge the reception to their ideas and listen to the diversity within the party.

Clarifying Party Images: Taxes and Programs

While the parties struggle with how much to stress social issues and the diversity of views among their members, in recent years each party has tried to establish more consistent images before the electorate.[19] Their long-term policy positioning has become clearer. Republicans have consistently argued that taxes are too high and have consistently sought to reduce them. Reducing the taxes that high income earners pay has been a persistent concern. Critics portray this as catering to the affluent out of self-interest and because the well-to-do provide them campaign contributions.

Republicans do not see that logic. They see tax cuts as part of an interpretative narrative of how the economy will work to generate more jobs. In their view taxes are burdens that discourage entrepreneurs from investing in business activities. Government regulations further discourage and inhibit investments because they present obstacles to taking action to create or expand businesses. Corporate taxes that are too high discourage large businesses from bringing profits into the United States, leaving less money to invest in businesses. The solution is lower taxes, lower taxes in particular on high income earners and their investments, and fewer government regulations.[20] The clear implication is that government actions can have a negative impact on economic growth and job creation. As a result of this view of the economy and government the party has adopted a consistent and persistent position that taxes must be cut. When George Bush was president he pushed through major tax cuts, even while launching wars in Afghanistan and Iraq. The logic was that tax cuts would spur economic growth, more jobs, and more tax revenue. When the economy went into a serious slump in 2008, Republicans advocated tax cuts. As the economy grew only gradually in 2010–2012 their proposal was tax cuts as a way to stimulate economic activity.

This advocacy of reducing taxes means there may be less revenue. Some within the party argue that the cuts will eventually stimulate the economy and will generate more tax revenue. But many argue that regardless of revenue implications, government is doing too much and needs to cut taxes. This has clear implications for the multitude of programs that government supports—Medicare, Medicaid, welfare, food stamps, grants to attend

college. The accompanying argument is that we cannot afford these programs. The government spends more than it receives and we have no choice
but to cut the programs. The policy image is increasingly clear to voters.
If they want to support a party that is anti-government and pro tax cuts
they should vote Republican. The periodic flare-up of social conservatism
issues sometimes distracts (while shoring up support among that part of their
base) from this clarity.

Democrats have also sought to establish a clear party image. Over years
the party has shed its southern base and now has a party that is consistently
more liberal than in prior decades. The party has sought to present an image
as concerned about those struggling in American society. They have
supported Medicare and Medicaid as necessary to provide health care to a
wide array of Americans. They have supported expansion of Pell grants,
which provide a grant for college attendance that does not have to be paid
back. They have consistently opposed the tax cuts of Republicans on the
grounds that they do not require the affluent to pay their fair share. They
have supported expansion of the Earned Income Tax Credit benefit. They
have sought to maintain programs like Food Stamps.

But Democrats have been unsure just how much to appear as liberal.
They have two anxieties. While they have supported all of the above programs, they worry about being labeled as simply in favor of redistribution.
Republicans have advocated a message of individual responsibility, which
resonates with Americans, and Democrats worry that they will look like
they believe in "a hand out and not a hand up." Their concern is that they
not convey an image to the middle class that they are taking their money
and simply giving it to those with lower incomes. For that reason, many
voted to limit welfare benefits in 1996. Prior to this revision, many welfare
recipients could stay on welfare for years. How much of that occurred was
a matter of dispute, but the party found defending that possibility very
difficult.

They have also been plagued by the existence of large deficits in recent
years. To Democrats these are a result of the large tax cuts passed by
Republicans in the early years of the Bush administration. But they face
the reality that the tax cuts have been in place for years now, and there are
large deficits. Republicans argue that we cannot afford many programs and
Democrats are faced with arguing for tax increases at a time when incomes
are not growing. They know the other party will seek to portray them as
fiscally irresponsible and as increasing the debt of the United States. While
the party wants to focus on the needs of people and the importance of
investing in them for the future, they also want to look like they have a
plan for containing deficits. Their response has been to advocate for
increasing taxes on the most affluent and some cuts in programs.

This balancing act was evident in passing the Affordable Health Care Act.
Democrats were trying to present themselves as concerned about those
without health care, as dealing with the growing cost of health care and

how much of its income it is consuming, but as concerned about how much their program would cost. They claimed the program would lower costs and that their estimates indicated the legislation would eventually save money. The narrative the Republicans have presented to voters is appealing to many: lower taxes and less government will stimulate growth. Democrats have sought to counter with arguments about the needs of people and fairness of tax burdens.

The attempt to balance different constituencies within a party is not without its costs. Barack Obama spent much of 2009 and 2010 speaking of attempting to work with Republicans, even as Republicans were uniting in opposition to his legislation[21] and Senate Minority leader Mitch McConnell said his sole goal was to defeat Obama. President Obama's concern was presumably to avoid looking like a strident liberal, partisan president in an effort to win over independents for the 2012 re-election bid. That moderation has its consequences, however. As 2011 unfolded, Obama heard more and more grumbling that he was not liberal enough, had compromised too much, and was not presenting the liberal case and was not opposing Republicans enough. This image has consequences. Those liberals who voted for Obama in 2008 were apparently less enthusiastic and were less willing to work for him and donate money.[22] For whatever reasons, during 2011 Obama moved to oppose and criticize publicly Republican initiatives. To return to the matters discussed in Chapter Eight, partisans are more likely to work for, contribute to, and vote for a party's candidate. With an election approaching, Obama was facing the issue of "mobilizing the base" versus moving to the middle. It is an ongoing challenge for each party. Defining a clear agenda motivates the most committed. It also can alienate the independents who do not like strident partisanship. Being partisan may disappoint many voters, but it activates others.

11 Disparaging the Other Party

Short-Term Strategies

While parties continually assess and adjust their positioning on policy positions, they also engage in an endless process (or "game" to some) of trying to convey to voters their doubts about the competence or ethics of the other party. The challenge is to convince the electorate that the other party cannot be trusted to handle the country's problems. To parties this is a rational part of the process of convincing the electorate that there is a difference between the parties. To return to issues of the context within which parties operate, most of the public is not following politics very much. They know few details of policy disputes. They follow events sporadically. The media does not cover policy disputes in much detail and it is difficult to get the media to explain the logic and specifics of policy proposals. They will, however, cover controversies and scandals. The lack of voter attention provides an opportunity to use specific instances to reinforce the beliefs of their base and to try to convince independents that the other party is not to be trusted. Sometimes these junctures provide an opportunity to also stress a substantive position, but often the focus is just on the competence and ethics of those executing party policies.

These behaviors also carry their risks. While one party may see an opportunity, taking advantage of it means adopting a critical and negative stance that may alienate as many as it attracts. The base may see the approach as confirming their suspicions about the other party, but independents and moderates just want problems solved and do not like what they see as partisan bickering. An approach of relentless criticism wears out voters who want solutions. But if the case can be made effectively that the other party has serious problems, it may be worth the gamble.

Competency Issues

Much of the public has one objective. They want problems addressed and resolved. Party leaders know that a crucial part of their arsenal in party battles is to convince the public that the other party is incompetent, that they cannot be trusted to handle problems. If that can be established, then presumably the electorate will reject the other side. During 1930 through to 1932, Democrats worked very hard to try to convince voters that Republicans had no answers to the Great Depression. Democrats provided little in the way of a coherent plan, but the issue of the capabilities of Republicans was crucial.

The efforts to question the competency of the other party are endless. Pollsters regularly ask voters which party they trust to handle various policy situations such as the economy, energy, or foreign policy.[1] The reactions of voters and their sense of which party "would do a better job dealing with . . ." are important when it comes to elections. Again, voters do not know policy details. They are making general judgments about the plausibility of a party's arguments on the basis of limited information.

When Democrats held the House of Representatives and Ronald Reagan was president there were numerous hearings in which Democrats were using their majority status to try to find cases where the Reagan administration had handled something poorly. In the sprawl of federal agencies it is not difficult to find something handled badly. When Bill Clinton was president Republicans gained control of the House in the 1994 elections and held it for the remainder of the Clinton administration. They used that control to launch hearings about alleged corruption or incompetence within the Clinton administration.

Following 9/11, Democrats found it very difficult to vote against the launching of wars in Afghanistan and Iraq by the Bush administration. The nation had been attacked and there was a sense that these countries might be a threat and there should be some retaliation. When the invasion of Iraq in March 2003 appeared to go well it became even more difficult to criticize the effort. Then it became clear that there were no weapons of mass destruction in Iraq, which had been one of the primary rationales for attacking Iraq. This raised the issue of the competency of the intelligence being gathered or the ability to interpret it in an objective way. Over time stories began to emerge of questionable management of the subsequent war effort. There were stories of waste, of incompetent political appointees, and poor coordination of efforts among agencies seeking to change the nation. While Democrats were reluctant to question the war, they found it easier to question whether the Bush administration was competent to manage the war effort. These developments were followed by Hurricane Katrina and its devastating impact on New Orleans. George Bush complimented his chief administrator by saying "Heck of a job, Brownie," but stories emerged about slow and ineffective responses. Democrats were able to mount a relentless criticism that the Bush administration was driven by ideology and not competence.

Republicans returned the favor in 2011 when the limit on how much the federal government could borrow had to be raised. As noted earlier it provided an opportunity for Republicans to reinforce their identity of favoring less government and limited government. But it also was an opportunity to make a simple argument that deficits were very high, total debt was rising, and President Obama had no plan to deal with what Republicans argued was a fundamental problem and a serious threat to the future of the nation. Obama's ratings on handling the deficit had been slipping since early 2009 and this was an opportunity to draw a contrast.[2] Enough Republicans eventually agreed to raise the debt limit to enact the change, but it was an opportunity to make their case that they were the only party willing to tackle a serious problem.

This conflict also illustrates the ambiguities that occur when trying to assess the impact of efforts by one party to disparage the plans and competence of the other party. The stance against raising the deficit was a major decision regarding the party's image, a situation they had anticipated and planned for.[3] The stalemate allowed Republicans to establish an image as opposed to ever-growing deficits. As a party stakes out a criticism of the other the hope is that voters will approve of their efforts and see them as more capable of handling the problem. The results were mixed. As the conflict ended, however, the electorate did not see anyone involved in it positively. When asked in polls of July 2011 (Table 11.1) whether they approved or disapproved of how various actors handled the controversy, the percentage disapproving was higher than those approving for President Obama, Speaker of the House John Boehner, and Majority Leader of the Senate Harry Reid. All three major actors were judged more negative than positive. Obama had higher approval ratings, but he still had more disapprove than approve. When asked whether the actors were putting their own political interests first or the country's, Republicans received by far the worst judgment with 72 percent saying they put their political interests first and only 24 percent the country's interests. For President Obama, 49 percent saw him as acting in his political interest and 47 percent as acting for the country. But while these results suggest Republicans lost in the showdown, when asked who they trusted to handle the deficit situation, 46 percent chose Republican leaders in Congress and 43 percent chose Obama. As is often the case, each side could find something in poll results to reassure them that their approach to the issue was working. While the public does not like these exchanges, they are part of the battle to shape voters' perceptions of what are important issues and which party is most capable of handling them. The debates may seem shallow to many, but the goal of a party is to establish broad competency differences before an electorate that pays limited attention.

Finally, the issue of gas prices presents another example of how parties seek to exploit events to try to disparage the opposition. When George W. Bush was president, gas prices rose from about $1.70 per gallon to $3.34 in 2008.[4] This resulted in relentless charges by Democrats that the Bush administration had no energy policy and was mismanaging the issue. Prices dipped and then rose again. Now it was Republicans' turn to disparage Obama's handling of gas prices. A poll indicated that 65 percent of Americans disapproved of his handling of gas prices and 26 percent approved.[5] Long-term data indicated that the real price (adjusted for inflation) had not

Table 11.1 The Deficit Battle of 2011: Public Reactions[a]

Please tell me whether you approve or disapprove of the way each of the following handled the negotiations to raise the federal debt ceiling. How about . . . ? (July 27, 2011)	*Approve*	*Disapprove*	*No Opinion*
President Barack Obama	41	49	10
Speaker John Boehner	31	48	21
Senate Majority Leader Harry Reid	23	52	25
Based on what you know or have read about their approach to the debt ceiling negotiations, do you think each of the following is putting their own political interests first, or putting the country's best interests first? How about . . .? (July 17, 2011)	*Own Political Interests First*	*Country's Best Interests First*	*No Opinion*
Republicans in Congress	72	24	4
Democrats in Congress	65	31	4
President Barack Obama	49	47	3
Who do you trust more to handle the issues concerning the federal budget deficit and the federal debt ceiling—President Barack Obama or the Republican leaders in Congress? (July 10, 2011)	*President Barack Obama*	*Republican Leaders in Congress*	*No Opinion*
	43	46	11

a Gallup Poll, "Federal Budget Deficit," ND., www.gallup.com/poll/147626/Federal-Budget-Deficit.aspx.

changed as much over time, that consumers were spending only 3–4 percent of their household income on gas from 2000 to 2012, and that much of the price increase was driven by demand from the growing economies elsewhere, such as China.[6] Nonetheless the issue provided an opportunity for both parties to criticize the competence of the other party. Again, the public does not like these critiques, but they are part of the efforts of each party to define the capabilities of the other.

Ethics Issues

Another way to persuade the public of the limitations of the other party is to try to find cases of ethical violations. The public may not understand complex policy choices and the media may not cover such debates, but scandals will get the attention of the media and voters. When Newt Gingrich was attempting to win a majority for Republicans in the House of Representatives in the late 1980s, he needed something to convince Americans that Democrats, after decades of holding power, had grown too comfortable with power and were corrupt. During this time the Speaker of the House, Jim Wright, had an arrangement for the publication of a book by him. Gingrich charged that the book was being bought in large bulk quantities by benefactors as a way to provide Wright with additional income and that the arrangement violated the ethics rules of Congress. Wright was eventually forced to resign and Gingrich was able to use the incident to label Democrats as corrupt.[7]

During the presidency of Bill Clinton, Republicans were faced with a politician who seemed adept at fending off their efforts to significantly cut government programs. When it emerged in 1998 that Clinton had a sexual relationship with an intern, Monica Lewinsky, it generated huge media coverage and eventually resulted in impeachment by the House of Representatives for perjury by Clinton on the issue and a trial in the Senate, where he was acquitted. While the prosecution of this issue by Republicans received strong support among Republicans, it did not by independents and Democrats and the incident had a limited effect on Clinton's overall job approval.[8]

When George W. Bush was president Democrats wanted very much to find some ethics issues to damage the reputation of Republicans. There were questions about the interpretation of pre-war intelligence about Iraq, about the awarding of contracts to companies to clean up the aftermath of Hurricane Katrina, and about the leaking to the public of the status of a CIA worker in retaliation for criticisms by her husband about the Iraq War. Democrats criticized these matters continually and the incidents played a role in damaging the public's perception of the Bush administration.[9]

Republicans held the House of Representatives following the 2010 elections and they pursued the case of a loan of $535 million to an energy firm by the Obama administration. The loan had been intended to help a struggling green technology energy firm, but the firm failed in late 2011.[10] The Republicans were able to use their control of committees to conduct an investigation into whether the firm had received preferential treatment because owners of the firm were well connected with administrative officials and had spent large sums lobbying Members of Congress.[11]

These efforts will continue. Again, many voters want an effective government that addresses problems. To the extent that one party can pin the labels of incompetence and corruption on the other party, those voters who just want problems dealt with and do not want to hear about ethics violations will vote at lower rates for the party seen as having problems. Just as with negative ads, the public does not like the game of continual charges between the parties, but they do shape voters' views of the parties.

12 Democracy and the Continuous Campaign

The goal of a political party is to win a majority that gives them control of both houses of Congress and the presidency. Our hope is that the process of pursuing that majority contributes to the democratic process. That is, they listen to the concerns of voters, sort through the diversity of opinions expressed and present us with policy proposals to respond to our concerns. Each party subjects the other party's proposals to public criticism, pointing out the flaws with their opponents' ideas. We are told who is likely to benefit and what effects the policies are likely to have. We, busy with our own lives, get some overview of how we might see the policy options being presented to us. An election is held and if a party wins a majority they can assume they have a basis for taking the actions they proposed. We as voters watch what a party does. The other party also watches and provides critiques of what is being done, alerting us to the flaws of their opponents. We can then render our judgment about what has been done in the next election. This process should make the concerns of voters—or at least a majority of them—central as policy decisions are made. The premise of a democracy, that voters matter, should be fulfilled.

We have numerous historical examples of this process playing out. In 2006 and 2008 voters were unhappy with President George Bush and the policies of his administration and Democrats acquired control of the Presidency, and the House and Senate. With the economy not improving and many unhappy over bailouts for the finance industry and the passage of the Affordable Health Care Act, in 2010 Democrats lost the House and their majority in the Senate was diminished. Democrats were sent a message that many voters were unhappy.

While we have examples of how the process works, the day-to-day behavior of parties seems far from the ideal we hold of the role of parties. We encounter simplistic slogans that may connect with a value we hold and touch an emotion but don't seem to enlighten us much about the policy issue. During a recent campaign the phrase "drill, baby, drill" was widely repeated. It reflected the view that we could find more domestic energy sources and reduce the cost of energy and our dependence on foreign sources. While it captured a sentiment, it left most of us with no sense of where this would occur, what environmental dangers might accompany drilling, how much energy might be generated and how fast it would occur.

We also encounter endless criticism of the other party over matters large and small. We encounter stubborn party leaders who oppose compromise and seek various means to slow down or stop policy proposals from the other party. Hearings are held to try to find a problem with the other party. Strategists are continually searching for incidents of malfeasance or corruption by those appointed by the other party. It is discouraging and alienating to many.

These behaviors, however, make sense, given the political context within which parties operate. To again repeat earlier material, voters are not terribly engaged with politics. They do not study issues and do not pay a great deal of attention. Parties know that. They do not react with dismay about the interest and knowledge of the electorate (though they may in private), but they focus on how to create an identity for themselves and their opponents before this marginally attentive electorate. They have to simplify and they have to repeat messages again and again because attention is sporadic. They have to criticize their opponents and establish that they are wrong. While the Affordable Health Care Act was being considered, Mitch McConnell, the minority leader in the Senate, argued to his conference that they could not have any Republican vote for the legislation because then Democrats would claim (with even one Republican vote) that it was bipartisan and must be good. Voters who were not paying attention would not look up how many Republicans that involved.[1] McConnell was operating with an awareness of the role of simplification and the awareness of voters. His apparent presumption was that he had to use this juncture to send a clear signal to voters that, amid all the policy detail debates, Republicans found something thoroughly wrong with the legislation.

Ultimately, do all these behaviors serve democracy? As annoying and disconcerting as they are, they do. Regardless of whether a party has a majority or is searching for one, each is continually aware of the need to listen to what voters are saying. Even the true-believing ideologues realize they must sometimes temper their beliefs in response to what polls, focus groups, and election results are telling them. The need to face voters makes politicians think about what matters to voters. A party may successfully frame an issue well enough to stifle opposition for a while, as Republicans did with the "War on Terror" theme in the mid 2000s. Democrats were reluctant to criticize the war effort, but eventually events made criticism easier and voting sentiment shifted. Republicans had to cope with the rising discontent with how foreign policy issues were being handled. The process of voters assessing policies, forming judgments, and politicians having to deal with them may be slower than we might wish, but it does occur.

Do the slogans of parties serve the process? It should be noted that there is considerable trial and error on the part of strategists in forming these slogans. Each party has some core beliefs and it is trying to find a way to frame an issue that reflects both their core values and public concerns. They may try several approaches before they hit one that combines these matters. We tend to forget the experiments or trial balloons of phrases that went nowhere with the public. If strategists do find a combination of values–concerns, their slogans are a way of connecting with those voters who might share their views and want the issue discussed in those terms. That helps get an issue on the agenda and represent concerns. When George Bush presented his No Child Left Behind legislation in the early 2000s and continually spoke of accountability he was able to combine a value of conservatives (schools should not just get more money without being accountable—a value and concern of many) with the concern about the performance of schools AND the principle of equal opportunity in a society that espouses that belief. It was a framing that served to convey concerns and structure public debate.

Does the endless criticism of the other party and the search for malfeasance and ethics violations help the democratic process? The virtue of these behaviors is that each party knows the other is searching for information to use against the other. That makes a party think about appointing people who are competent and about conceiving, implementing, and managing programs in a way that is defensible in understandable terms to the public. It means presuming transparency and anticipating how things will look to the public. It means taking ethics issue seriously so there will not be a scandal the other party can use against them as an election approaches.

The process may not always be pleasing to watch. Parties make many mistakes in judging their support, in how they attack their opponents, and in their depth and duration of opposition to the other party. They may distort issues to try to get voters to see them in their way. Reading the public and how positions will work is a very inexact science. But the parties are responsive to shifts in opinion. They do serve the democratic process.

Notes

1 Democracy and the Ideal Role of Political Parties

1. E. E. Schattschneider, *Party Government* (New York: Holt, Rinehart and Winston, 1942), 1.
2. Joe Klein, "Middle of the Road," *Time*, October 24, 2011, 30.
3. Frank Newport, "Americans Again Call for Compromise in Washington," Gallup Poll, September 26, 2011; available at: www.gallup.com/poll/149699/Americans-Again-Call-for-Compromise-Washington.aspx.
4. Gordon S. Wood, *The Creation of the American Republic, 1776–1787* (Chapel Hill University of North Carolina Press, 1969), 344–389; and, Edmund S. Morgan, *Inventing the People: The Rise of Popular Sovereignty in England and America* (New York: W. W. Norton, 1998). This faith in "the people" was an abstraction for much of American history. There were many who doubted the legitimacy and capabilities of non-landowners, immigrants, women, blacks, and those convicted of a felony. The right to vote has expanded only gradually over time. See Alexander Keyssar, *The Right to Vote: The Contested History of Democracy in the United States* (New York: Basic Books, 2000).
5. John H. Aldrich, *Why Parties?: The Origin and Transformation of Party Politics in America* (Chicago: University of Chicago Press, 1995); and John H. Aldrich, *Why Parties? A Second Look* (Chicago: University of Chicago Press, 2011).
6. E. E. Schattschneider, *The Semi-Sovereign People: A Realist's View of Democracy in America* (New York: Holt, Rinehart, and Winston, 1960).
7. Lizabeth Cohen, *Making a New Deal: Industrial Workers in Chicago, 1919–1939* (New York: Cambridge University Press, 1990); and, David Plotke, *Building a Democratic Political Order: Reshaping American Liberalism in the 1930s and 1940s* (New York: Cambridge University Press, 1996).
8. James Davison Hunter, *Culture Wars: The Struggle to Control the Family, Art, Education, Law, and Politics in America* (New York: Basic Books, 1992).
9. Greg D. Adams, "Abortion: Evidence of an Issue Evolution," *American Journal of Political Science*, Vol. 41, No. 3 (1997), 718–737.
10. David Rohde and John Aldrich, "Consequences of Electoral and Institutional Change: The Evolution of Conditional Party Government in the U.S. House of Representatives," in Jeffrey M. Stonecash, Editor, *New Directions in American Political Parties* (New York: Routledge, 2010), 234–250.
11. Richard Beeman, *Plain, Honest Men: The Making of the American Constitution* (New York: Random House, 2009); and, Gordon S. Wood, *The Creation of the American Republic, 1776–1787* (Chapel Hill: University of North Carolina Press, 1969).

12. James MacCregor Burns, *The Deadlock of Democracy* (New York: Marion Boyars Publishers, 1954); and Morris P. Fiorina, *Divided Government*, Second Edition (Boston: Allyn and Bacon, 1996).

13. Arthur M. Schlesinger, *The Crisis of the Old Order: 1919–1933* (New York: Mariner Books, 2003); and Arthur M. Schlesinger, *The Coming of the New Deal, 1933–1935* (New York: Mariner Books, 2003).

14. Howard L. Reiter and Jeffrey M. Stonecash, *Counter-Realignment: Political Change in the Northeast* (New York: Cambridge University Press, 2010), 55–80.

15. G. Calvin Mackenzie and Robert Weisbrot, *The Liberal Hour: Washington and the Politics of Change in the 1960s* (New York: Penguin Press, 2008).

16. Theda Skocpol, *Boomerang: Health Care Reform and the Turn against Government* (New York: W.W. Norton, 1997).

17. Dan Balz and Ronald Brownstein, *Storming the Gates: Protest Politics and the Republican Revival* (Boston: Little Brown, 1996).

18. Gary C. Jacobson, *A Divider, Not a Uniter: George W. Bush and the American People* (New York: Pearson/Longman, 2007).

19. How politicians interpret an election will be taken up later. This case provides an example of how differently a politician can interpret results. President Bush argued that the results meant he had to do a better job creating peace and a stable government in Iraq and chose to send more troops to Iraq.

2 Enduring Doubts about Political Parties

1. Many Members keep a separate apartment or home in Washington, which they must pay for themselves.

2. A portrait of politicians to this effect that has had considerable influence is Morris P. Fiorina, *Congress: Keystone of the Washington Establishment* (New Haven, CT: Yale University Press, 1977).

3. Anthony Downs, *An Economic Theory of Democracy* (New York: Harper and Row, 1957), 28.

4. Eric Lichtblau, "Economic Downturn Took a Detour at Capitol Hill," *New York Times*, December 26, 2011, A1; and, Peter Whoriskey, "Growing Wealth Widens Distance between Lawmakers and Constituents," *Washington Post*, December 26, 2011: www.washingtonpost.com/business/economy/growing-wealth-widens-distance-between-lawmakers-and-constituents/2011/12/05/gIQAR7D6IP_story.html?wpisrc=nl_politics.

5. David R. Mayhew, "Congressional Elections: The Case of the Vanishing Marginals," *Polity*, Vol. 6, No. 3 (Spring 1974), 295–317; David R. Mayhew, *The Electoral Connection* (New Haven, CT: Yale University Press, 1974).

6. Walter D. Burnham, "Insulation and Responsiveness in Congressional Elections," *Political Science Quarterly*, Vol. 90, No. 3 (Fall 1975), 411–413.

7. Edward T. Tufte "The Relationship between Seats and Votes in Two-Party Systems," *American Political Science Review*, Vol. 67, No. 2 (June 1973).

8. Kevin Phillips, *Wealth and Democracy* (New York: Broadway Books, 2002), 201–248 and 317–346; and, Larry M. Bartels, *Unequal Democracy: The Political Economy of the New Gilded Age* (New York: Russell Sage Foundation, and Princeton, NJ: Princeton University Press, 2008); and Lawrence Lessig, *Republic, Lost: How Money Corrupts Congress—and a Plan to Stop It* (New York: Twelve, 2011). For an accompanying video about the issue of money in politics see: www.amazon.com/gp/mpd/permalink/m1eyx10ern0gn1/ref=ent_fb_link.

9. James K. Coyne and John H. Fund, *Cleaning House: America's Campaign for Term Limits* (New York: Regnery, 1992); George F. Will, *Restoration: Congress, Term Limits, and the Recovery of Deliberative Democracy* (New York: Free Press, 1993).

10. For background on the progressive movement, which was the initial sponsor of many of these reforms, see Richard Hofstadter, *The Age of Reform* (New York: Vintage, 1960); Rosenblum, *On the Side of Angels*, 165–209.

11. Thad Kousser, *Term Limits and the Dismantling of State Legislative Professionalism* (New York: Cambridge University Press, 2004); and, Rick Farmer, Christopher Z. Mooney, Richard J. Powell, and John C. Green, *Legislating Without Experience: Case Studies in State Legislative Term Limits* (Lanham, MD: Lexington Books, 2007). For information on efforts to establish term limits in the states see: www.termlimits.org/.

12. Dennis R. Judd and Todd Swanstrom, *City Politics*, Eighth Edition (New York: Longman, 2011).

13. Louis Hartz, *The Liberal Tradition in America* (New York: Harcourt, Brace, 1955).

14. Jeffrey M. Jones, "Americans See U.S. as Exceptional; 37% Doubt Obama Does," Gallup Poll, December 22, 2010: www.gallup.com/poll/145358/Americans-Exceptional-Doubt-Obama.aspx. In that poll, the percentage agreeing America is exceptional by party identification was: Democrats 73, Independents 77, Republicans 91.

15. Seymour Martin Lipset, *American Exceptionalism: A Double-Edged Sword* (New York: W.W. Norton, 2007).

16. Alexis de Tocqueville, *Democracy in America*, translated by George Lawrence, edited by J.P. Mayer (Garden City: Anchor / Doubleday Anchor, 1969), 177.

17. Nancy L. Rosenblum, *On the Side of Angels: An Appreciation of Parties and Partisanship* (Princeton, NJ: Princeton University Press, 2008), 12.

18. James Madison, Alexander Hamilton, and John Jay, No. 10, *The Federalist Papers*, edited by Isaac Kramnick (New York: Viking Penguin, 1987), 124.

19. Morris P. Fiorina, with Samuel J. Abrams, *Disconnect: The Breakdown of Representation in American Politics* (Norman: University of Oklahoma Press, 2009), xix and 12.

20. Jonathan Weisman, "After Many Tough Choices, the Choice to Quit," *New York Times*, March 1, 2012, A1.

21. Frank Bruni, "Snowe's Sad Retreat," *New York Times*, Sunday Review, March 4, 2012, 3.

22. Erik Eckholm, "Poll Finds Divisions Over Requiring Coverage," *New York Times*, March 2, 2012, A15.

23. Joe Klein, "Stuck in the Middle," *Time*, October 10, 2011, 25.

24. Thomas Frank, *What's the Matter with Kansas?* (New York: Metropolitan Books, 2004

25. Markus Prior, *Post-Broadcast Democracy* (New York: Cambridge University Press, 2007).

26. Jonathan M. Ladd, *Why Americans Hate the Media and How It Matters* (Princeton, NJ: Princeton University Press, 2012).

27. Pew Research Center for the People & the Press, "Growing Number of Americans Say Obama is a Muslim Religion," August 19, 2010: http://pewresearch.org/pubs/1701/poll-obama-muslim-christian-church-out-of-politics-political-leaders-religious.

28. David Paul Kuhn, "The Partisan Industrial Complex," Real Clear Politics: www.realclearpolitics.com/articles/2009/09/24/the_partisan_industrial_complex__98407.html.

29. Dana Millbank, "Roe v. Wade's Greedy Offspring," *Washington Post*, January 17, 2012: www.washingtonpost.com/opinions/roe-v-wade-and-the-dishonest-industry-it-spawned/2012/01/17/gIQAaf5T6P_story.html.

30. Joshua Green, "The Rove Presidency," *Atlantic Monthly*, November, 2007: www.theatlantic.com/magazine/archive/2007/09/the-rove-presidency/6132/; Ronald Brownstein, *The Second Civil War: How Extreme Partisanship has Paralyzed Washington and Polarized America* (New York: Penguin Press, 2007), 287–288.

31. Morris P. Fiorina with Samuel J. Abrams and Jeremy C. Pope, *Culture War?: The Myth of a Polarized America* (New York: Longman, 2011), 79–108.

32. John Aldrich, "Partisan Polarization and Satisfaction with Democracy," presented at the 2012 Southern Political Science Association Meetings, New Orleans, January, 2012.

33. Amy Gutmann and Dennis Thompson, *Why Deliberative Democracy?* (Princeton, NJ: Princeton University Press, 2004).

34. Rosenblum, *On the Side of* Angels, 165–253.

35. Jacobson, *A Divider, Not a Uniter*, 7.

36. The Gallup Poll: www.gallup.com/poll/124922/Presidential-Approval-Center.aspx.

37. Stephen Ansolabehere and Shanto Iyengar, *Going Negative: How Political Advertisements Shrink and Polarize the Electorate* (New York: Free Press, 1995). For a recent review of this issue see Bryce Corrigan and Ted Brader, "Campaign Advertising: Reassessing the Impact of Campaign Ads on Political Behavior," in Stephen K. Medvic, Editor, *New Directions in Campaigns and Elections* (New York: Routledge, 2011), 79–97.

38. Juliet Eilperin, *Fight Club Politics: How Partisanship is Poisoning the House of Representatives* (Lanham, MD: Rowman & Littlefield, 2006); Brownstein, *The Second Civil War*; and, George Packer, "The Empty Chamber: Just how broken is the Senate?" *The New Yorker*, August 9, 2010: www.newyorker.com/reporting/2010/08/09/100809fa_fact_packer.

39. Rosenblum, *On the Side of* Angels, 325–335.

40. Jeffrey M. Jones, "Republican, Democratic Party Images Equally Negative Approval of Republicans, Democrats in Congress at or near record lows," September 30, 2011: www.gallup.com/poll/149795/Republican-Democratic-Party-Images-Equally-Negative.aspx.

41. Pew Research Center for the People and the Press, "Public Trust in Government, 1958–2010," www.people-press.org/2010/04/18/public-trust-in-government-1958–2010/.

42. Frank Newport, "Congress Ends 2011 with Record-Low 11% Approval: Annual average for 2011, 17%, also lowest in Gallup history," December 19, 2011: www.gallup.com/poll/151628/Congress-Ends-2011-Record-Low-Approval.aspx.

43. Lydia Saad, "Americans Express Historic Negativity Toward U.S. Government," September 26, 2011: www.gallup.com/poll/149678/Americans-Express-Historic-Negativity-Toward-Government.aspx.

44. Jeffrey M. Jones, "Record-High 40% of Americans Identify as Independents in '11," January 9, 2012: www.gallup.com/poll/151943/Record-High-Americans-Identify-Independents.aspx.

45. Nicol C. Rae, *Conservative Reformers: The Republican Freshmen and the Lessons of the 104th Congress* (Armonk, NY: M.E. Sharpe, 1998), 96–130.

46. Newport, "Americans Again Call for Compromise in Washington," Gallup Poll, September 26, 2011.

47. Joe Klein, "Stuck in the Middle," *Time*, October 10, 2011, 25.

3 Notions of Party and Conflict

1. For a thorough review of these efforts, see: Rosenblum, *On the Side of Angels*.
2. The concerns here are the challenges that parties play in contributing to representation and decision-making. As such, many of the rules and practices surrounding parties will get little attention. There are several excellent textbooks on American political parties that provide background material on party rules and practices (organization, state regulations of them, diversity of state parties, nomination of executive and legislative candidates, elections and campaign finance, party identification in the electorate, and the behavior of elected party members in legislatures. John F. Bibby, *Politics, Parties and Elections in America*, Sixth Edition (Belmont, California: Wadsworth, 2007); Marjorie R. Hershey, *Party Politics in America*, Fourteenth Edition (New York: Longman, 2011); Marc J. Hetherington and William J. Keefe, *Parties, Politics, and Public Policy in America*, Tenth Edition (Washington, D.C.: CQ Press, 2007); and L. Sandy Maisel and Mark D. Brewer, *Parties and Elections in America*, Sixth Edition (New York: Rowman & Littlefield, 2011).
3. A good overview of this argument is presented in Aldrich, *Why Parties? A Second Look*, 255–323. For an overview of this literature see Jeffrey M. Stonecash, "Political Science and the Study of Parties: Sorting out Interpretations of Party Response," in Mark D. Brewer and L. Sandy Maisel, Editors, *The Parties Respond*, Fifth Edition (Boulder, CO: Westview Press, 2012), 1–23.
4. J. P. Monroe, *The Political Party Matrix: The Persistence of Organization*. Albany: State University of New York Press, 2001); Paul S. Herrnson, "The Roles of Party Organization, Party-Connected Committees, and Party Allies in Elections," *Journal of Politics*, Vol. 71, No. 4 (October 2009), 1207–1224; Seth E. Masket, *No Middle Ground: How Informal Party Organizations Control Nominations and Polarize Legislatures* (Ann Arbor: University of Michigan Press, 2009). For the party efforts that were crucial in recruiting House Members who would stand for fiscal conservativism see Dennis Brady, Alec MacGillis, and Lori Montgomery, "Origins of the Debt Showdown," *Washington Post,* August 6, 2011: www.washingtonpost.com/business/economy/origins-of-the-debt-showdown/2011/08/03/gIQA9uqIzI_story.html.
5. See, for example, Matt Grossman and Casey B. K. Dominguez, "Party Coalitions and Interest Group Networks," *American Politics Research*, Vol. 37, No. 5 (September 2009), 767–800; Gregory Koger, Seth Masket, and Hans Noel, "Cooperative Party Factions in American Politics," *American Politics Research*, Vol. 38, No. 1 (January 2010), 33–53; Gregory Koger, Seth E. Masket, and Hans Noel, "Partisan Webs: Information Exchange and Party Networks," *British Journal of Political Science*, Vol. 39, No. 3 (July 2009), 633–653; Casey B. K. Dominguez, "Does the Party Matter? Endorsements in Congressional Primaries," *Political Research Quarterly*, Vol. 64, No. 3 (September 2011), 534–544; and, Richard M. Skinner, Seth E. Masket, and David A. Dulio, "527 Committees and the Political Party Network," *American Politics Research*, Vol. 40, No. 1 (January, 2012), 60–84.
6. For an interesting argument about who in this network is most important see: Kathleen Bawn, Marty Cohen, David Karol, Seth Masket, Hans Noel, and John Zaller, *A Theory of Political Parties*, 2011, Unpublished: www9.georgetown.edu/faculty/hcn4/Downloads/ToP%20October%205.pdf.
7. Hartz, *The Liberal Tradition in America*.
8. Michael Delli Carpini and Scott Keeter, *What Americans Know about Politics and Why it Matters* (New Haven, CT: Yale University Press, 1996).

9. The most prominent statements of these views are in Morris P. Fiorina and Samuel J. Abrams, "Political Polarization in the American Public," *Annual Review of Political Science*, Vol. 11, 2008, 563–588; Fiorina with Abrams, *Disconnect*; and Fiorina with Abrams and Pope, *Culture War?*

10. Nolan McCarty, Keith T. Poole, and Howard Rosenthal, *Polarized America: The Dance of Ideology and Unequal Riches* (Cambridge, MA: The MIT Press, 2006); Earl Black and Merle Black, *Divided America: The Ferocious Power Struggle in American Politics* (New York: Simon and Schuster, 2007); Donald C. Baumer and Howard J. Gold, *Parties, Polarization, and Democracy in the United States* (Boulder, CO: Paradigm Publishers, 2010); and, Alan I. Abramowitz, *The Polarized Public: Why American Government Is So Dysfunctional* (New York: Pearson, 2013).

11. For an overview of the issue of who is divided and how that has changed over time, see Geoffrey C. Layman, Thomas M. Carsey, and Julianna Menasce Horowitz, "Party Polarization in American Politics: Characteristics, Causes, and Consequences," *Annual Review of Political Science*, Vol. 9, 2006, 83–110; and, Geoffrey C. Layman, Thomas M. Carsey, John C. Green, Richard Herrera, and Rosalyn Cooperman, "Party Polarization, Party Commitment, and Conflict Extension among American Party Activists," *American Political Science Review*, Vol. 104, No. 2 (May 2010), 324–346.

12. Brian D. Feinstein and Eric Schickler, "Platforms and Partners: The Civil Rights Realignment Reconsidered," *Studies in American Political Development*, Vol. 22 (Spring 2008), 115–16.

13. For an overview of these social trends and party responses see Mark D. Brewer and Jeffrey M. Stonecash, *Split: Class and Cultural Divisions in American Politics* (Washington, D.C.: CQ Press, 2007).

14. David W. Rohde, *Parties and Leaders in the Postreform House* (Chicago: University of Chicago Press, 1991); Gary C. Jacobson, "Party Polarization in National Politics: The Electoral Connection," in Jon R. Bond and Richard Fleisher, Editors, *Polarized Politics: Congress and the President in a Partisan Era* (Washington, D.C.: Congressional Quarterly Press, 2000), 9–30; Gary C. Jacobson, "Party Polarization in Presidential Support: The Electoral Connection," *Congress and the Presidency*, Vol. 30, No. 1 (Spring, 2003), 1–36; Nelson W. Polsby, *How Congress Evolves: Social Bases of Institutional Change* (New York: Oxford University Press, 2004); Sean M. Theriault, *Party Polarization in Congress* (New York: Cambridge University Press, 2008); and, Mark D. Brewer and Jeffrey M. Stonecash, *The Dynamics of American Political Parties* (New York: Cambridge University Press, 2009).

15. Alan I. Abramowitz and Kyle L. Saunders, "Ideological Realignments in the U.S. Electorate," *Journal of Politics*, Vol. 60, No. 3 (August 1998), 634–652; and, Alan I. Abramowitz and Kyle L. Saunders, "Exploring the Bases of Partisanship in the American Electorate: Social Identity vs. Ideology," *Political Research Quarterly*, Vol. 59, No. 2 (June 2006), 175–187.

16. The response of those who see less conflict is that people are just sorting themselves out as elites who pursue their own arguments and positions. Fiorina, *Cultural War*, 61–70; and Mathew Levendusky, *Partisan Sort* (Chicago: University of Chicago Press, 2009). These arguments have some plausibility in that they suggest a set of observers watching conflict in Washington and a relatively passive adjustment. In doing so, the "sorting" argument largely dismisses the idea of a party as a network of committed individuals and groups seeking to recruit individuals to their side.

17. Geoffrey C. Layman and Thomas M. Carsey, "Party Polarization and 'Conflict Extension' in the American Electorate," *American Journal of Political Science*, Vol. 46,

No. 4 (October 2002), 786–802; and, Mark D. Brewer, "The Rise of Partisanship and the Expansion of Partisan Conflict within the American Electorate," *Political Research Quarterly*, Vol. 58, No. 2 (June 2005), 219–229.

18. Mark D. Brewer and Jeffrey M. Stonecash, "Individual vs. Societal Responsibility: The Root of Partisan and Ideological Conflict," presented at the 2012 Southern Political Science Association Meetings, New Orleans, January.

19. Marc J. Hetherington and Jonathan Weiler, *Authoritarianism and Polarization in American Politics* (New York: Cambridge University Press, 2009).

20. Charles Murray, *Losing Ground: American Social Policy, 1950–1980*, Tenth Anniversary Edition (New York: Basic Books, 1994); and, Marvin Olasky, *The Tragedy of American Compassion* (Washington, D.C.: Regnery Publishing, 1992).

21. Alan I. Abramowitz, *The Disappearing Center: Engaged Citizens, Polarization, and American Democracy* (New Haven, CT: Yale University Press, 2010).

22. Jeffrey M. Stonecash, *Parties Matter: Realignment and the Return of Partisanship* (Boulder, CO: Lynne Rienner, 2006).

23. E. J. Dionne, *They Only Look Dead* (New York: Touchstone, 1997).

24. Thomas M. Carsey and Geoffrey C. Layman, "Changing Sides or Changing Minds? Party Identification and Policy Preferences in the American Electorate," *American Journal of Political Science*, Vol. 50, No. 2 (April, 2006), 464–477. Levendusky, *Partisan Sort*, argues that "voters typically shift their ideology to fit with their party identification; ideology-driven party exit (changing one's party to fit with one's ideology) occurs in only a narrow set of circumstances" (p. 3).

25. Edward G. Carmines and James A. Stimson, *Issue Evolution* (Princeton, NJ: Princeton University Press, 1989); and, Kerry L. Haynie and Candis S. Watts, "Blacks and the Democratic Party: A Resilient Coalition," in Jeffrey M. Stonecash, Editor, *New Directions in American Political Parties* (New York: Routledge, 2010), 93–109.

26. Jeffrey M. Stonecash, *Class and Party in American Politics* (Boulder, CO: Westview Press, 2000); Bartels, *Unequal Democracy*; and, Stonecash, "Class in American Politics," in Jeffrey M. Stonecash, Editor, *New Directions in American Political Parties* (New York: Routledge, 2010), 110–125.

27. Abramowitz, *The Disappearing Center*, 34–61.

28. Geoffrey C. Layman, "'Cultural Wars' in the American Party System," *American Politics Quarterly*, Vol. 27, No. 1 (January 1999), 89–121; and Geoffrey C. Layman, *The Great Divide: Religious and Cultural Conflict in American Party Politics* (New York: Columbia University Press, 2001); and Laura R. Olson, "Religion, Moralism, and the Cultural Wars: Competing Moral Visions," in Jeffrey M. Stonecash, Editor, *New Directions in American Political Parties* (New York: Routledge, 2010), 148–165.

29. William Julius Wilson, *When Work Disappears: The World of the New Urban Poor* (Chicago: University of Chicago Press, 1996).

30. Charles Murray, *Coming Apart: The State of White America, 1960–2010* (New York: Crown Forum, 2012).

31. For an analysis of how presidential candidates have shifted their positions over time see David Karol, *Party Position Change in American Politics: Coalition Management* (New York: Cambridge University Press, 2009).

4 Shifting Electoral Bases

1. David Burner, *The Politics of Provincialism: The Democratic Party in Transition* (New York: Alfred Knopf, 1968); Elizabeth Sanders, *Roots of Reform: Farmers, Workers, and the American State* (Chicago: University of Chicago Press, 1999); Douglas B.

Craig, *After Wilson: The Struggle for the Democratic Party, 1920–1934* (Chapel Hill: University of North Carolina Press, 1992).

2. James L. Sundquist, *Dynamics of the Party System: Alignment and Realignment of Political Parties in the United States, Revised Edition* (Washington, D.C.: Brookings Institution, 1983), 198–239.

3. Cohen, *Making a New Deal*; and, Plotke, *Building a Democratic Political Order*.

4. Sidney M. Milkis and Jerome M. Mileur, Editors, *The Great Society and the High Tide of Liberalism* (Amherst: University of Massachusetts Press, 2006); and, Mackenzie and Weisbrot, *The Liberal Hour*.

5. Carmines and Stimson, *Issue Evolution*.

6. Rick Perlstein, *Before the Storm* (New York: Hill and Wang, 2001).

7. Kevin Phillips, *The Emerging Republican Majority* (New York: Anchor, 1969).

8. Nicole Mellow, *The State of Disunion: Regional Sources of Modern American Partisanship* (Baltimore: Johns Hopkins University Press, 2008).

9. Merle Black and Earl Black, *Politics and Society in the South* (Cambridge, MA: Harvard University Press, 1987); Merle Black and Earl Black, *The Rise of Southern Republicans* (Cambridge, MA: Harvard University Press, 2002).

10. Reiter and Stonecash, *Counter-Realignment*; and, Alan Ware, *The Democratic Party Moves North* (New York: Cambridge University Press, 2006).

11. Northeast is Maine, New Hampshire, Vermont, Massachusetts, Rhode Island, Connecticut, New York, New Jersey, Delaware, and Pennsylvania. The Midwest is Ohio, Indiana, Illinois, Michigan, Wisconsin, and Minnesota. The South is Virginia, North Carolina, South Carolina, Georgia, Florida, Alabama, Mississippi, Louisiana, Texas, Tennessee, and Kentucky. The remaining states are Other.

12. William Crotty, *American Parties in Decline*, Second Edition (Boston: Little Brown, 1984); Martin P. Wattenberg, *The Decline of American Political Parties 1952–1988* (Cambridge, MA: Harvard University Press, 1990); Martin P. Wattenberg, *The Rise of Candidate-Centered Politics: Presidential Elections of the 1980s* (Cambridge, MA: Harvard University Press, 1991); Martin P. Wattenberg, *The Decline of American Political Parties, 1952–1996* (Cambridge, MA: Harvard University Press, 1998); and, David Menefee-Libey, *The Triumph of Candidate-Centered Politics* (New York: Chatham House, 2000).

13. Jeffrey M. Stonecash, *Party Pursuits and the Presidential–House Election Connection, 1900–2008* (New York: Cambridge University Press, 2013).

14. Larry M. Bartels, "Partisanship and Voting Behavior, 1952–1996," *American Journal of Political Science*, Vol. 44, No. 1 (January 2000), 35–49; Marc J. Hetherington, "Resurgent Mass Partisanship: The Role of Elite Polarization?" *American Political Science Review*, 95 (September 2001), 619–32; and, Stonecash, *Parties Matter*.

5 Conflicting Interpretations of Change

1. Mayhew, "Congressional Elections;" and, Mayhew, *The Electoral Connection*.

2. For a review of these changes, see Aldrich, *Why Parties? A Second Look*.

3. Crotty, *American Parties in Decline*.

4. Martin P. Wattenberg, "The Decline of Political Partisanship in the United States: Negativity or Neutrality?" *American Political Science Review*, Vol. 75, No. 4 (December 1981), 941–950; Wattenberg, *The Decline of American Political Parties 1952–1988*; and, Wattenberg, *The Rise of Candidate-Centered Politics*.

5. Bruce E. Cain, John A. Ferejohn, and Morris P. Fiorina, "The Constituency Basis of the Personal Vote for U.S. Representatives and British Members of Parliament,"

American Political Science Review, Vol. 78, No. 1 (March 1984), 110–125; and, Bruce E. Cain, John A. Ferejohn, and Morris P. Fiorina, *The Personal Vote: Constituency Service and Electoral Independence* (Cambridge, MA: Harvard University Press, 1990).

6. Stonecash, *Party Pursuits and the Presidential–House Election Connection, 1900–2008.*
7. Menefee-Libey, *The Triumph of Candidate-Centered Politics*; and, Eric McGhee, "National Tides and Local Results in US House Elections," *British Journal of Political Science,* Vol. 38, No. 4 (October 2008).
8. Paul Herrnson, *Congressional Elections: Campaigning at Home and Washington*, Fifth Edition (Washington, D.C.: CQ Press, 2008), 1–70; John Sides, Daron Shaw, Matt Grossman, and Keena Lipsitz, *Campaigns & Elections: Rules, Reality, Strategy, and Choice* (New York: W.W. Norton, 2012), 68–75.
9. D. Sunshine Hillygus and Todd G. Shields, *The Persuadable Voter* (Princeton, NJ: Princeton University Press, 2008).
10. Ware, *The Democratic Party Moves North.*
11. Carmines and Stimson, *Issue Evolution*; and, Haynie and Watts, "Blacks and the Democratic Party."
12. Black and Black, *Politics and Society in the South*; and, Joseph Aistrup, *The Southern Strategy Revisited* (Lexington: University of Kentucky Press, 1996).
13. Rogers M. Smith and Desmond S. King, "Racial Orders in American Political Development," *American Political Science Review*, Vol. 99, No. 1 (February 2005), 75–92; and Desmond S. King and Rogers M. Smith, *Still a House Divided* (Princeton, NJ: Princeton University Press, 2011).
14. Thomas B. and Mary D. Edsall, *Chain Reaction: The Impact of Race, Rights, and Taxes on American Politics* (New York: W.W. Norton, 1991); Gordon MacInnes, *Wrong, for all the Right Reasons: How White Liberals Have Been Undone by Race* (New York: New York University Press, 1996).
15. David Paul Kuhn, *The Neglected Voter: White Men and the Democratic Dilemma* (New York: Palgrave Macmillan, 2007).
16. For a review of these trends see Brewer and Stonecash, *Split,* 87–110.
17. Hunter, *Culture Wars.*
18. Hetherington and Weiler, *Authoritarianism and Polarization in American Politics.*
19. Dionne, *They Only Look Dead.*
20. Frank, *What's the Matter with Kansas?*
21. Not everyone has agreed that there is a cultural war occurring. See Fiorina with Abrams and Pope, *Culture War?*
22. Everett Carll Ladd, "Liberalism Turned Upside Down: The Inversion of the New Deal Order," *Political Science Quarterly*, Vol. 91, No. 4 (Winter, 1976–1977), 577–600; and, Everett Carll Ladd, "Is Election '84 Really a Class Struggle?" *Public Opinion* (April / May, 1984), 41–51.
23. Stanley Greenberg, *Middle Class Dreams* (New York: Times Books, 1996).
24. David Brooks, "Workers of the World, Unite!" *New York Times*, January 3, 2011, A21.
25. Richard W. Stevenson, "Tough Fight Ahead for White Blue Collar Votes," *New York Times*, January 14, 2011, A12; and, see John Harwood, "Obama's Tax Policy Targets Rising Sector of His Base; The Affluent," *New York Times*, February 20, 2012, A10.
26. Stonecash, *Class and Party in American Politics*; Bartels, *Unequal Democracy*; Stonecash, "Class in American Politics"; and Byron E. Shafer and Richard Johnston, *The End of Southern Exceptionalism: Class, Race, and Partisan Change in the Postwar South* (Cambridge, MA: Harvard University Press, 2006).

27. To further complicate the issue, there has been a long tradition within sociology of defining class in terms of occupational position because of the presumption that occupation defines your relative position in society. Others use self-identification in a survey. The approach to defining class can produce different results, making it even harder for a strategist to reach a conclusion.

28. David Brooks, "The Class War Before Palin," *New York Times*, October 10, 2008, A33.

29. Rebekah Liscio, Jeffrey M. Stonecash, and Mark D. Brewer, "Unintended Consequences: Republican Strategy and Winning and Losing Voters," in John C. Green and Daniel J. Coffey, Editors, *The State of the Parties*, Sixth Edition (New York: Rowman & Littlefield, 2010), 255–270.

6   The Lack of a Majority

1. For works that grapple with this issue see Scott C. James, *Presidents, Parties, and the State: A Party System Perspective on Democratic Regulatory Choice* (New York: Cambridge University Press, 2000); Jeffrey M. Stonecash, "The Electoral College and Democratic Responsiveness," in Gary Baugh, Editor, *Electoral College Reform: Challenges and Possibilities* (Burlington, VT: Ashgate, 2010), 65–76; Marty Cohen, David Karol, Hans Noel, and John Zaller, *The Party Decides: Presidential Nominations Before and After Reform* (Chicago: University of Chicago Press, 2008); and, Karol, *Party Position Change in American Politics*.

2. Leaners can be added to initial identifiers because research indicates that leaners tend to behave in much the same way as self-identified partisans. See Bruce E. Keith, David B. Magleby, Candice J. Nelson, Elizabeth Orr, Mark C. Westlye, and Raymond E. Wolfinger, *The Myth of the Independent Voter* (Berkeley: University of California Press, 1992).

3. As an example of an analysis that concluded that neither party had a majority in the mid-1990s see: Everett Carll Ladd, "1996 Vote: the 'No Majority' Realignment Continues," *Political Science Quarterly*, Vol. 112, No. 1 (Spring, 1997), 1–18.

4. Figure 6.4 data are from: Lydia Saad, "Conservatives Remain the Largest Ideological Group in U.S.: Overall, the nation has grown more polarized over the past decade," January 12, 2012: www.gallup.com/poll/152021/Conservatives-Remain-Largest-Ideological-Group.aspx. These Gallup data also indicate that a substantial percentage of the Democratic Party identifies itself as conservative.

5. The issue of what Americans really want from government has generated considerable research. For examples of studies that explore this, see: Benjamin I. Page, *The Rational Public: Fifty Years of Trends in Americans' Policy Preferences* (Chicago: University of Chicago Press, 1992); Benjamin I. Page and Lawrence R. Jacobs, *Class War? What Americans Really Think about Economic Inequality* (Chicago: University of Chicago Press, 2009); and, Suzanne Mettler, *The Submerged State: How Invisible Government Policies Undermine American Democracy* (Chicago: University of Chicago Press, 2011).

6. Karen Tumulty, "Recent debate over contraception comes as GOP loses gains among women," *Washington Post*, March 9, 2012: www.washingtonpost.com/politics/republicans-suffer-among-female-voters/2012/03/08/gIQANzfM1R_story.html; Susan Saulny, "Centrist Women Tell of Disenchantment With G.O.P.," *New York Times*, March 10, 2012: www.nytimes.com/2012/03/11/us/politics/centrist-women-tell-of-disenchantment-with-gop.html?_r=1&hp; and, Robert Pear, "House G.O.P. Hesitates on Birth Control Fight," *New York Times*, March 16, 2012, A16.

7 Continuing Social Change and Events

1. Sheldon Danziger and Peter Gottschalk, *America Unequal* (Cambridge, MA: Harvard University Press, 1995), 53. Incomes are first grouped from lowest to highest, and then broken into groups of tenths. The percentage increases in incomes within each category, from the beginning to the end of the era, are then computed.
2. Congressional Budget Office, *Trends in the Distribution of Household Income Between 1979 and 2007*, October 2011: www.cbo.gov/doc.cfm?index=12485.
3. Lisa A. Keister, *Wealth in America* (New York: Cambridge University Press, 2000); Lisa A. Keister, *Getting Rich: America's New Rich and How they Got That Way* (New York: Cambridge University Press, 2005); and, Pew Research Center, *Wealth Gaps Rise to Record Highs Between Whites, Blacks, and Hispanics*, Washington, D.C., July 26, 2011.
4. Michael Barone, *Hard America Soft America: Competition vs. Coddling and the Battle for the Nation's Future* (New York: Three Rivers Press, 2004); and Arthur C. Brooks, *The Battle: How the Fight Between Free Enterprise and Big Government Will Shape America's Future* (New York: Basic Books, 2010).
5. These data are as of 2009 and are from The Tax Foundation: www.taxfoundation. org/taxdata/show/27235.html.
6. For examples of this argument see Jacob S. Hacker, *The Great Risk Shift: The New Economic Insecurity and the Decline of the American Dream* (New York: Oxford, 2008); Jacob S. Hacker and Paul Pierson, *Off Center: The Republican Revolution and the Evolution of Democracy* (Yale University Press, 2005); and, Jacob S. Hacker and Paul Pierson, *Winner-Take-All Politics: How Washington Made the Rich Richer—and Turned its Back on the Middle Class* (New York: Simon and Schuster, 2010).
7. Page and Jacobs, *Class War?* 25–48.
8. Rich Morin, "Rising Share of Americans See Conflict Between Rich and Poor," Pew Research Center, January 11, 2012: www.pewsocialtrends.org/2012/01/11/rising-share-of-americans-see-conflict-between-rich-and-poor/?src=prc-headline.
9. Frank Newport, "Americans Divided on Whether U.S. Economic System Is Unfair: More than 6 in 10 say it is fair to them personally," Gallup Poll, January 25, 2012: www.gallup.com/poll/152186/Americans-Divided-Whether-Economic-System-Unfair.aspx.
10. Andrew Kohut, "Don't Mind the Gap," *New York Times,* January 26, 2012: http://campaignstops.blogs.nytimes.com/2012/01/26/dont-mind-the-gap/?scp=1&sq=Don't%20mind%20the%20gap&st=cse.
11. Brewer and Stonecash, *Split*, 77.
12. There is also the argument that some of the inequality is because government gives away many benefits to the affluent through hidden tax breaks, which few people are aware of, but do not like when informed of them. In this view inequality could become an issue because of who benefits from tax breaks. See Mettler, *The Submerged State*.
13. Jill H. Wilson, "Trends in U.S. Immigration," The Brookings Institution, March 24, 2009: www.brookings.edu/speeches/2009/0324_immigration_wilson.aspx. There are also many data available at the Migration Policy Institute: www.migration information.org/datahub/historicaltrends.cfm#history.
14. Samuel P. Huntington, *Who Are We? The Challenges to America's National Identity* (New York: Simon and Schuster, 2005).
15. Jeffrey Passel and D'Vera Cohn, "Unauthorized Immigrant Population: National and State Trends, 2010," Pew Hispanic Center, February 1, 2011: www.pewhispanic.

org/2011/02/01/unauthorized-immigrant-population-brnational-and-state-trends-2010/.

16. Phillips, *The Emerging Republican Majority*.

17. Marika Dunn and Jane Junn, "Immigration and Political Parties," in Jeffrey M. Stonecash, Editor, *New Directions in American Political Parties* (New York: Routledge, 2010), 166–185.

18. For analyses arguing that the Democratic appeal to minorities hurt the Democratic Party see Edsall and Edsall, *Chain Reaction* and Kuhn, *The Neglected Voter*.

19. Kirk Johnson, "G.O.P. Plays to Hispanic Fears About Economy," *New York Times*, March 16, 2012, A1.

20. Hetherington and Weiler, *Authoritarianism and Polarization in American Politics*.

21. Hillygus and Shields, *The Persuadable Voter*.

22. Frank, *What's the Matter with Kansas?*

23. Brooks, "The Class War Before Palin;" and, Liscio, Stonecash, and Brewer, "Unintended Consequences: Republican Strategy and Winning and Losing Voters."

24. Jeffrey M. Jones, "Support for Legal Gay Relations Hits New High: Sixty-four percent believe they should be legal," Gallup Poll, May 25, 2011: www.gallup.com/poll/147785/Support-Legal-Gay-Relations-Hits-New-High.aspx.

25. Frank Newport, "For First Time, Majority of Americans Favor Legal Gay Marriage: Republicans and older Americans remain opposed," May 20, 2011: www.gallup.com/poll/147662/First-Time-Majority-Americans-Favor-Legal-Gay-Marriage.aspx; and, Andrew Gelman, Jeffrey Lax, and Justin Phillips, "Over Time, a Gay Marriage Groundswell," *New York Times*, August 21, 2010: www.nytimes.com/2010/08/22/weekinreview/22gay.html?scp=1&sq=Andrew%20Gelman&st=cse.

26. Gallup Poll, "Abortion," nd.: www.gallup.com/poll/1576/Abortion.aspx#1.

27. Anita Pugliese and Julie Ray, "Fewer Americans, Europeans View Global Warming as a Threat Worldwide, 42% See Serious Risk, Similar to 2007–2008," April 20, 2011: www.gallup.com/poll/147203/Fewer-Americans-Europeans-View-Global-Warming-Threat.aspx; and, Riley E. Dunlap, "Climate-Change Views: Republican–Democratic Gaps Expand Sharp divergence on whether the effects of global warming are yet evident," May 29, 2008: www.gallup.com/poll/107569/Climate Change-Views-RepublicanDemocratic-Gaps-Expand.aspx.

28. Michael Ettlinger and Michael Linden, "Who's to Blame for the Deficit Numbers?" August 25, 2009: www.americanprogress.org/issues/2009/08/deficit_numbers.html; and, Quinnipiac University Poll, "Voters Blame Bush Over Obama 2–1 for Financial Mess," July 14, 2011: www.quinnipiac.edu/institutes-and-centers/polling-institute/national/release-detail?ReleaseID=1624.

29. Frank Newport, "Americans Blame Wasteful Government Spending for Deficit: Prefer cutting spending over raising taxes as way for Congress to reduce deficit," April 29, 2011: www.gallup.com/poll/147338/Americans-Blame-Wasteful-Government-Spending-Deficit.aspx.

30. Pew Research Center, "More Blame Wars than Domestic Spending or Tax Cuts for Nation's Debt: Jobs are top economic worry, deficit concerns rise," June 7, 2011: www.people-press.org/2011/06/07/more-blame-wars-than-domestic-spending-or-tax-cuts-for-nations-debt/.

31. Gallup Poll, "Federal Budget Deficit," May 29, 2008, www.gallup.com/poll/147626/Federal-Budget-Deficit.aspx#1.

8 Voters, Partisanship and the Media

1. Pew Research Center, "What the Public Knows—In Words and Pictures," November 7, 2011: www.people-press.org/2011/11/07/what-the-public-knows-in-words-and-pictures/?src=prc-headline.
2. Jeffrey M. Stonecash, "The 2010 Elections: Party Pursuits, Voter Perceptions, and the Chancy Game of Politics," *The Forum*, Vol. 8, Issue 4 (December 2010): www.degruyter.com/view/j/for.2011.8.4/for.2011.8.4.1407/for.2011.8.4.1407.xml?format =INT.
3. Andrew Hacker, "The Next Election: The Surprising Reality," *New York Review of Books*, August 18, 2011, 78–80.
4. CNN Exit Polls: www.cnn.com/ELECTION/2008/results/polls/#USH00p1; and, www.cnn.com/ELECTION/2010/results/polls/#USH00p1.
5. Larry M. Bartels, "Partisanship and Voting Behavior, 1952–1996," *American Journal of Political Science*, Vol. 44, No. 1 (January 2000), 35–49; Hetherington, "Resurgent Mass Partisanship;" and, Stonecash*, Parties Matter.*
6. Green, "The Rove Presidency."
7. Prior, *Post-Broadcast Democracy*; and, Danny Hayes, "Party Communication in a Transformed Media Age," in Jeffrey M. Stonecash, Editor, *New Directions in Political Parties* (New York: Routledge, 2010), 44–62.
8. Pew Research Center for the People and the Press, "Internet Gains on Television as Public's Main News Source," January 4, 2011: www.people-press.org/2011/01/04/internet-gains-on-television-as-publics-main-news-source/2/; Pew Research Center for the People and the Press, "Cable Leads the Pack as Campaign News Source," February 7, 2012: www.people-press.org/2012/02/07/cable-leads-the-pack-as-campaign-news-source/.
9. Pew Research Center, "Partisanship and Cable News Audiences," October 30, 2009: http://pewresearch.org/pubs/1395/partisanship-fox-news-and—other-cable-news-audiences; Pew Research Center, "Americans Spending More Time Following the News," September 12, 2010: www.people-press.org/2010/09/12/section-1-watching-reading-and-listening-to-the-news/.
10. Jennifer Steinhauer and Helene Cooper, "Democrats see Benefits in Battling Republicans on Contraception Issue," *New York Times*, February 28, 2012, A12.
11. Reed Abelson, "Catholic Hospitals Expand, Religious Strings Attached," *New York Times*, February 20, 2012: www.nytimes.com/2012/02/21/health/policy/growth-of-catholic-hospitals-may-limit-access-to-reproductive-care.html.
12. Diana Dwyre, "Party Organization and Mobilization of Resources: Evolution, Reinvention, and Survival," in Jeffrey M. Stonecash, Editor, *New Directions in American Political Parties* (New York: Routledge, 2010), 63–90.
13. Bartels, *Unequal Democracy*.

10 Pursuing Coalitions and an Identity: Long-Term Strategies

1. Philip A. Klinkner, *The Losing Parties: Out-Party National Committees, 1956–1993* (New Haven, CT: Yale University Press, 1993); Robin Kolodny and Diana Dwyre, "Party-Orchestrated Activities for Legislative Party Goals," *Party Politics*, Vol. 4, No. 3 (July, 1998), 275–295; and Karol, *Party Position in American Politics*; and, Jim Ruthenberg and Jeff Zeleny, "Democrats Outrun by a 2-Year G.O.P. Comeback Plan," *New York Times*, November 3, 2010.

2. Donald P. Green, Bradley Palmquist, and Eric Shickler, *Partisan Hearts and Minds: Political Parties and the Social Identities of Voters* (New Haven, CT: Yale University Press, 2002).

3. For more detailed analyses, see Karol, *Party Position Change in American* Politics; and, Stonecash, *Party Pursuits and the Presidential–House Election Connection, 1900–2008*.

4. Sanders, *Roots of Reform*.

5. Burner, *The Politics of Provincialism: The Democratic Party in Transition*; and, Craig, *After Wilson*.

6. Nicol Rae, *The Decline and Fall of Liberal Republicans from 1952 to the Present* (New York: Oxford University Press, 1989); and, Donald T. Critchlow, *The Conservative Ascendancy* (Cambridge, MA: Harvard University Press, 2007).

7. Perlstein, *Before the Storm*.

8. Reiter and Stonecash, *Counter Realignment*.

9. Phillips, *The Emerging Republican Majority*.

10. Rick Perlstein, *Nixonland: The Rise of a President and the Fracturing of America* (New York: Scribner, 2007); and, Robert Mason, *Richard Nixon and the Quest for a New Majority* (Chapel Hill: University of North Carolina Press, 2004).

11. Black and Black, *The Rise of Southern Republicans*, 246.

12. Shafer and Johnston, *The End of Southern Exceptionalism*.

13. Lydia Saad, "Congress Gets Thumbs Down for Stepping Into Schiavo Case," Gallup Poll, April 7, 2005: www.gallup.com/poll/15541/Congress-Gets-Thumbs-Down-Stepping-Into-Schiavo-Case.aspx; Frank Newport, "The Terri Schiavo Case in Review," April 1, 2005: www.gallup.com/poll/15475/Terri-Schiavo-Case-Review.aspx.

14. Thomas E. Patterson, *Out of Order* (New York: Alfred Knopf, 1993).

15. Ruy A. Teixeira and Joel Rogers, *America's Forgotten Majority: Why the White Working Class Still Matters* (New York: Basic Books, 2000).

16. Jon F. Hale, "The Making of the New Democrats," *Political Science Quarterly*, Vol. 110. No. 2 (Summer 1995), 207–232; William Galston, "The Future of the Democratic Party." *The Brookings Review* (Winter, 1985), 16–24; William Galston and Elaine C. Kamarck, "The Politics of Evasion: Democrats and the Presidency." Washington, D.C.: The Progressive Policy Institute. 2 (May, 1989), 195–216; and, Kenneth S. Baer, *Reinventing Democrats: The Politics of Liberalism from Reagan to Clinton* (Lawrence: University Press of Kansas, 2000).

17. Mark Landler, "On Gay Rights, Obama Lets Surrogates Lead," *New York Times*, December 30, 2011: www.nytimes.com/2011/12/31/us/politics/on-gay-rights-obama-lets-surrogates-take-the-lead.html.

18. David Remnick, "Obama and Gay Marriage," *The New Yorker*, June 22, 2011: www.newyorker.com/online/blogs/newsdesk/2011/06/obama-and-gay-marriage.html.

19. Mark D. Brewer, *Party Images in the American Electorate* (New York: Routledge, 2008).

20. Brooks, *The Battle*; and, Nicholas Wapshott, *Keynes Hayek: The Clash that Defined Modern Economics* (New York: W.W. Norton, 2011).

21. Jackie Calmes, "House Passes Stimulus Bill With No G.O.P. Votes," *New York Times*, January 28, 2009: www.nytimes.com/2009/01/29/us/politics/29obama.html.

22. Nicholas Confessore, "Small Donors Are Slow to Return to the Obama Fold," *New York Times*, September 24, 2011: www.nytimes.com/2011/09/25/us/politics/small-donors-slow-to-return-to-obama-fold.html?_r=2&scp=3&sq=Obama%20fund%20raising&st=cse.

11 Disparaging the Other Party: Short-Term Strategies

1. Jeffrey Jones, "Neither Party Has Big Edge on Most Major U.S. Issues," Gallup Poll, April 29, 2011: www.gallup.com/poll/147332/Neither-Party-Big-Edge-Major-Issues.aspx.
2. Frank Newport, "Obama Gets Highest Approval on Iraq, Lowest on Deficit," Gallup Poll, September 17, 2009: www.gallup.com/poll/122981/Obama-Gets-Highest-Approval-Iraq-Lowest-Deficit.aspx.
3. Brady, MacGillis, and Montgomery, "Origins of the Debt Showdown."
4. "Gas Prices in Context," *Washington Post,* March 13, 2012: www.washington post.com/wp-srv/special/opinions/gas-prices/.
5. Dan Balz and Jon Cohen, "Gas Prices Sink Obama's Ratings on Economy, Bring Parity to Race for White House," *Washington Post,* March 12, 2012: www. washingtonpost.com/politics/gas-prices-sink-obamas-ratings-on-economy-bring-parity-to-race-for-white-house/2012/03/11/gIQAuhYO6R_story.html?hpid=z1.
6. Steve Mufson, "Voters Blame President for Gas Prices, Experts Say Not So Fast," *Washington Post,* March 13, 2012: www.washingtonpost.com/business/economy/voters-blame-president-for-gas-prices-experts-say-not-so-fast/2012/03/12/gIQ A8fsO8R_story.html?wpisrc=nl_headlines.
7. Gingrich later encountered his own problems with ethics issues and an admission that he was carrying on an affair with an assistant and eventually he was forced to resign as Speaker of the House of Representatives in 1999.
8. Gallup News Services, "Public Supports Censure, Not Removal," February 11, 1999: www.gallup.com/poll/4081/Public-Supports-Censure-Removal.aspx.
9. Gary Langer, "Poll: Ethical Issues Tar Bush Administration," ABC News, October 30, 2005: http://abcnews.go.com/Politics/PollVault/story?id=1264205.
10. Solyndra, *New York Times,* November 17, 2011: http://topics.nytimes.com/top/news/business/companies/solyndra/index.html?offset=0&s=newest.
11. Matthew Wald, "House Panel Votes to Subpoena Solyndra Documents," November 3, 2011: http://green.blogs.nytimes.com/2011/11/03/house-panel-votes-to-subpoena-solyndra-documents/?ref=solyndrahttp://green.blogs.nytimes.com/2011/11/03/house-panel-votes-to-subpoena-solyndra-documents/?ref=solyndra.

12 Democracy and the Continuous Campaign

1. Lawrence R. Jacobs and Theda Skocpol, *Health Care Reform and American Politics* (New York: Oxford University Press, 2010), 85–86.

Bibliography

Abelson, Reed. 2012. "Catholic Hospitals Expand, Religious Strings Attached," *New York Times*, February 20: www.nytimes.com/2012/02/21/health/policy/growth-of-catholic-hospitals-may-limit-access-to-reproductive-care.html.

Abramowitz, Alan I. 2010. "Ideological Realignment Among Voters." In Jeffrey M. Stonecash, Editor, *New Directions in American Political Parties*. New York: Routledge. 126–147.

——. 2010. *The Disappearing Center: Engaged Citizens, Polarization, and American Democracy*. New Haven, CT: Yale University Press.

——. 2013. *The Polarized Public: Why American Government Is So Dysfunctional*. New York: Pearson.

——, and Kyle L. Saunders. 1998. "Ideological Realignments in the U.S. Electorate." *Journal of Politics*, Vol. 60, No. 3 (August): 634–652.

——, ——. 2006. "Exploring the Bases of Partisanship in the American Electorate: Social Identity vs. Ideology." *Political Research Quarterly*. Vol. 59, No. 2 (June): 175–187.

Adams, Greg D. 1997. "Abortion: Evidence of an Issue Evolution," *American Journal of Political Science*, Vol. 41, No. 3: 718–737.

Aistrup, Joseph. 1996. *The Southern Strategy Revisited*. Lexington: University of Kentucky Press.

Aldrich, John. 1995. *Why Parties? The Origin and Transformation of Political Parties in America*. Chicago: University of Chicago Press.

——. 2008. "Partisan Polarization and Satisfaction with Democracy." Presented at the 2012 Southern Political Science Association Meetings. New Orleans. January.

——. 2011. *Why Parties? A Second Look*. Chicago: University of Chicago Press.

Ansolabehere, Stephen, and Shanto Iyengar. 1995. *Going Negative: How Political Advertisements Shrink and Polarize the Electorate*. New York: Free Press.

Baer, Kenneth S. 2000. *Reinventing Democrats: The Politics of Liberalism from Reagan to Clinton*. Lawrence: University Press of Kansas.

Balz, Dan, and Jon Cohen. 2012. "Gas Prices Sink Obama's Ratings on Economy, Bring Parity to Race for White House," *Washington Post,* March 12: www.washingtonpost.com/politics/gas-prices-sink-obamas-ratings-on-economy-bring-parity-to-race-for-white-house/2012/03/11/gIQAuhYO6R_story.html?hpid=z1.

Balz, Daniel J., and Ronald Brownstein. 1996. *Storming the Gates: Protest Politics and the Republican Revival*. Boston: Little, Brown, and Company.

Barone, Michael. 2004. *Hard America Soft America: Competition vs. Coddling and the Battle for the Nation's Future*. New York: Three Rivers Press.

Bartels, Larry M. 2000. "Partisanship and Voting Behavior, 1952–1996." *American Journal of Political Science*, Vol. 44, No. 1 (January): 35–49.

——. 2008. *Unequal Democracy: The Political Economy of the Gilded Age*. Princeton, NJ: Princeton University Press.

Baumer, Donald C., and Howard J. Gold. 2010. *Parties, Polarization, and Democracy in the United States*. Boulder, CO: Paradigm Publishers.

Bawn, Kathleen, Marty Cohen, David Karol, Seth Masket, Hans Noel, and John Zaller. 2011. *A Theory of Political Parties*. Unpublished: www9.georgetown.edu/faculty/hcn4/Downloads/ToP%20October%205.pdf

Beeman, Richard. 2009. *Plain, Honest Men: The Making of the American Constitution*. New York: Random House.

Bibby, John F. 2007. *Politics, Parties and Elections in America*. Sixth Edition. Belmont, CA: Wadsworth.

Binder, Sarah A. 2003. *Stalemate: Causes and Consequences of Legislative Gridlock*. Washington, D.C.: Brookings Institution.

Black, Earl, and Merle Black. 1987. *Politics and Society in the South*. Cambridge, MA: Harvard University Press.

——. 2002. *The Rise of Southern Republicans*. Cambridge, MA: Harvard University Press.

——. 2007. *Divided America: The Ferocious Power Struggle in American Politics*. New York: Simon and Schuster.

Brady, Dennis, Alec MacGillis, and Lori Montgomery, "Origins of the Debt Show-down," *Washington Post*, August 6, 2011: www.washingtonpost.com/business/economy/origins-of-the-debt-showdown/2011/08/03/gIQA9uqIzI_story.html.

Brewer, Mark D. 2005. "The Rise of Partisanship and the Expansion of Partisan Conflict within the American Electorate." *Political Research Quarterly*. Vol. 58, No. 2 (June): 219–229.

——. 2008. *Party Images in the American Electorate*. New York: Routledge.

Brewer, Mark D., and Jeffrey M. Stonecash. 2007. *Split: Class and Cultural Divides in American Politics*. Washington, D.C.: CQ Press.

——, ——. 2009. *The Dynamics of American Political Parties*. New York: Cambridge University Press.

Brooks, Arthur C. 2010. *The Battle: How the Fight Between Free Enterprise and Big Government Will Shape America's Future*. New York: Basic Books.

Brooks, David. 2008. "The Class War Before Palin," *New York Times*, October 10. A33.

——. 2011. "Workers of the World, Unite!" *New York Times*, January 3. A21.

Brownstein, Ronald. 2007. *The Second Civil War: How Extreme Partisanship Has Paralyzed Washington and Polarized America*. New York: Penguin Press.

Bruni, Frank. 2012. "Snowe's Sad Retreat," *New York Times*, Sunday Review, March 4, 2012, 3.

Burnham, Walter Dean. 1975. "Insulation and Responsiveness in Congressional Elections." *Political Science Quarterly*. Vol. 90, No. 3 (Fall): 411–35.

Burner, David. 1968. *The Politics of Provincialism: The Democratic Party in Transition*. New York: Alfred Knopf.

Burns, James MacGregor. 1954. *The Deadlock of Democracy*. New York: Marion Boyars Publishers.

Cain, Bruce E., John A. Ferejohn, and Morris P. Fiorina. 1984. "The Constituency Basis of the Personal Vote for U.S. Representatives and British Members of Parliament." *American Political Science Review*. Vol. 78, No. 1 (March): 110–125.

——. 1990. *The Personal Vote: Constituency Service and Electoral Independence.* Cambridge: Harvard University Press.

Calmes, Jackie. 2009. "House Passes Stimulus Bill With No G.O.P. Votes," *New York Times,* January 28, 2009: www.nytimes.com/2009/01/29/us/politics/29obama.html.

Carmines, Edward G., and James A. Stimson. 1989. *Issue Evolution: Race and the Transformation of American Politics.* Princeton, NJ: Princeton University Press.

Carpini, Michael Delli, and Scott Keeter. 1996. *What Americans Know about Politics and Why it Matters.* New Haven, CT: Yale University Press.

Carsey, Thomas M., and Geoffrey C. Layman. 2006. "Changing Sides or Changing Minds? Party Identification and Policy Preferences in the American Electorate." *American Journal of Political Science* 50 (April): 464–477.

CNN Exit Polls. N.d. www.cnn.com/ELECTION/2008/results/polls/#USH00p1; and, www.cnn.com/ELECTION/2010/results/polls/#USH00p1.

Cohen, Lizabeth. 1990. *Making a New Deal: Industrial Workers in Chicago, 1919–1939.* New York: Cambridge University Press.

Cohen, Marty, David Karol, Hans Noel, and John Zaller. 2008. *The Party Decides: Presidential Nominations Before and After Reform.* Chicago: University of Chicago Press.

Confessore, Nicholas. 2011. "Small Donors Are Slow to Return to the Obama Fold," *New York Times,* September 24: www.nytimes.com/2011/09/25/us/politics/small-donors-slow-to-return-to-obama-fold.html?_r=2&scp=3&sq=Obama%20fund%20raising&st=cse.

Congressional Budget Office. 2011. *Trends in the Distribution of Household Income Between 1979 and 2007,* October: www.cbo.gov/doc.cfm?index=12485.

Corrigan, Bryce, and Ted Brader. 2011. "Campaign Advertising: Reassessing the Impact of Campaign Ads on Political Behavior." In Stephen K. Medvic, Editor, *New Directions in Campaigns and Elections.* New York: Routledge. 79–97.

Coyne, James K., and John H. Fund. 1992. *Cleaning House: America's Campaign for Term Limits.* New York: Regnery.

Craig, Barbara Hinkson, and David M. O'Brien. 1993. *Abortion and American Politics.* Chatham, NJ: Chatham House Publishers, Inc.

Critchlow, Donald. 2007. *The Conservative Ascendancy.* Cambridge, MA: Harvard University Press.

Crotty, William. 1984. *American Parties in Decline.* Second Edition. Boston: Little, Brown, and CO.

Dalton, Russell J. 2012. *The Apartisan American: Dealignment and Changing Electoral Politics.* Washington, D.C.: CQ Press.

Danziger, Sheldon, and Peter Gottschalk. 1995. *America Unequal.* Cambridge, MA: Harvard University Press.

Dionne, E. J., Jr. 1997. *They Only Look Dead.* New York: Touchstone.

Dominguez, Casey B. K. 2011. "Does the Party Matter? Endorsements in Congressional Primaries." *Political Research Quarterly.* Vol. 64, No. 3 (September): 534–544.

Downs, Anthony. 1957. *An Economic Theory of Democracy.* New York: Harper and Row.

Dulio, David A. 2011. "The Impact of Political Consultants." In Stephen C. Craig and David B. Hills, Editors. *Electoral Challenge: Theory Meets Practice.* Second Edition. Washington, D.C.: CQ Press. 243–270.

Dunlap, Riley E. 2008. "Climate-Change Views: Republican–Democratic gaps expand sharp divergence on whether the effects of global warming are yet evident," Gallup Poll, May 29: www.gallup.com/poll/107569/ClimateChange-Views-Republican Democratic-Gaps-Expand.aspx.

Dunn, Marika, and Jane Junn. 2010. "Immigration and Political Parties." In Jeffrey M. Stonecash, Editor, *New Directions in American Political Parties*. New York: Routledge. 166–185.

Dwyre, Diana. 2010. "Party Organization and Mobilization of Resources: Evolution, Reinvention, and Survival." In Jeffrey M. Stonecash, Editor, *New Directions in American Political Parties*. New York: Routledge. 63–90.

Eckholm, Erik. 2012. "Poll Finds Divisions Over Requiring Coverage," *New York Times*, March 2. A15.

Edsall, Thomas Byrne, and Mary D. Edsall. 1991. *Chain Reaction: The Impact of Race, Rights, and Taxes on American Politics*. New York: W.W. Norton.

Eilperin, Juliet. 2006. *Fight Club Politics: How Partisanship is Poisoning the House of Representatives*. Lanham MD: Rowman and Littlefield.

Ettlinger, Michael, and Michael Linden. 2009. "Who's to Blame for the Deficit Numbers?" August 25: www.americanprogress.org/issues/2009/08/deficit_numbers.html.

Farmer, Rick, Christopher Z. Mooney, Richard J. Powell, and John C. Green. 2007. *Legislating Without Experience: Case Studies in State Legislative Term Limits*. Lanham MD: Lexington Books.

Feinstein, Brian D., and Eric Schickler. 2008. "Platforms and Partners: The Civil Rights Realignment Reconsidered." *Studies in American Political Development*. Vol. 22 (Spring): 115–116.

Ferejohn, John A. 1977. "On the Decline of Competition in Congressional Elections." *American Political Science Review*. Vol. 71, No. 1 (March): 166–176.

Fiorina, Morris P. 1977. *Congress: Keystone of the Washington Establishment*. New Haven, CT: Yale University Press.

——. 1992. *Divided Government*. Boston: Allyn and Bacon.

——. 1996. *Divided Government*. Second Edition. Boston: Allyn and Bacon.

——, and Samuel J. Abrams. 2008. "Political Polarization in the American Public." *Annual Review of Political Science*. Vol. 11: 563–588.

——, ——. 2009. *Disconnect: The Breakdown of Representation in American Politics*. Norman: University of Oklahoma Press.

——, ——, and Jeremy C. Pope. 2006. *Culture War? The Myth of a Polarized America*, Second Edition. New York: Pearson/Longman.

——, ——, and Jeremy C. Pope. 2011. *Culture War? The Myth of a Polarized America*, Third Edition. New York: Pearson/Longman.

Frank, Thomas. 2004. *What's the Matter with Kansas? How Conservatives Won the Heart of America*. New York: Metropolitan Books.

Gallup Poll. 1999. "Public Supports Censure, Not Removal," Gallup Poll, February 11: www.gallup.com/poll/4081/Public-Supports-Censure-Removal.aspx.

Gallup Poll. N.d. "Abortion," www.gallup.com/poll/1576/Abortion.aspx#1.

——. N.d. "Federal Budget Deficit," www.gallup.com/poll/147626/Federal-Budget-Deficit.aspx#1.

Galston, William. 1985. "The Future of the Democratic Party." *The Brookings Review* (Winter): 16–24.

——, and Elaine C. Kamarck. 1989. "The Politics of Evasion: Democrats and the Presidency." Washington, D.C.: The Progressive Policy Institute. 2 (May): 195–216.

Gelman, Andrew, Jeffrey Lax, and Justin Phillips. 2010. "Over Time, a Gay Marriage Groundswell," *New York Times*, August 21: www.nytimes.com/2010/08/22/weekinreview/22gay.html?scp=1&sq=Andrew%20Gelman&st=cse.

Green, Joshua. 2007. "The Rove Presidency," *Atlantic Monthly*, November: www.the atlantic.com/magazine/archive/2007/09/the-rove-presidency/6132/.

Green, Donald P., Bradley Palmquist, and Eric Shickler. 2002. *Partisan Hearts and Minds: Political Parties and the Social Identities of Voters*. New Haven, CT: Yale University Press.

Greenberg, Stanley B. 1996. *Middle Class Dreams: Politics and Power of the New American Majority*. New Haven, CT: Yale University Press.

Grossman, Matt, and Casey B. K. Dominguez. 2009. "Party Coalitions and Interest Group Networks." *American Politics Research*. Vol. 37, No. 5 (September): 767–800.

Gutmann, Amy, and Dennis Thompson. 2004. *Why Deliberative Democracy?* Princeton, NJ: Princeton University Press.

Hacker, Andrew. 2011. "The Next Election: The Surprising Reality," *New York Review of Books*, August 18: 78–80.

Hacker, Jacob S. 2008. *The Great Risk Shift: The New Economic Insecurity and the Decline of the American Dream*. New York: Oxford.

——, and Paul Pierson. 2005. *Off Center: The Republican Revolution and the Erosion of Democracy*. New Haven, CT: Yale University Press.

——, ——. 2010. *Winner-Take-All Politics: How Washington Made the Rich Richer—and Turned its Back on the Middle Class*. New York: Simon and Schuster.

Hale, Jon F. 1995. "The Making of the New Democrats." *Political Science Quarterly*. Vol. 110. No. 2: 207–232.

Hartz, Louis. 1955. *The Liberal Tradition in America*. New York: Harcourt, Brace.

Harwood, John. 2012. "Obama's Tax Policy Targets Rising Sector of His Base; The Affluent," *New York Times*, February 20. A10.

Hayes, Danny. 2010. "Party Communication in a Transformed Media Age." In Jeffrey M. Stonecash, Editor, *New Directions in Political Parties*. New York: Routledge. 44–62.

Haynie, Kerry L., and Candis S. Watts. 2010. "Blacks and the Democratic Party: A Resilient Coalition." In Jeffrey M. Stonecash, Editor, *New Directions in American Political Parties*. New York: Routledge. 93–109.

Herrnson, Paul S. 2008. *Congressional Elections: Campaigning at Home and in Washington*, Fifth Edition. Washington, D.C.: Congressional Quarterly Press.

——. 2009. "The Roles of Party Organization, Party-Connected Committees, and Party Allies in Elections." *Journal of Politics*. Vol. 71, No. 4 (October): 1207–1224.

Hershey, Marjorie Randon. 2009. *Party Politics in America*, Thirteenth Edition. New York: Pearson/Longman.

Hetherington, Marc J. 2001. "Resurgent Mass Partisanship: The Role of Elite Polarization?" *American Political Science Review*, Vol. 95, No. 3 (September): 619–32.

——, and Jonathan D. Weiler. 2009. *Authoritarianism and Polarization in American Politics*. Cambridge: Cambridge University Press.

——, and William J. Keefe. 2007. *Parties, Politics, and Public Policy in America*, Tenth Edition. Washington, D.C.: CQ Press.

Hillygus, D. Sunshine, and Todd G. Shields. 2008. *The Persuadable Voter: Wedge Issues in Presidential Campaigns*. Princeton, NJ: Princeton University Press.

Hofstadter, Richard. 1960. *The Age of Reform*. New York: Vintage.

Humes, Karen R., Nicholas A. Jones, and Roberto R. Ramirez. 2011. *Overview of Race and Hispanic Origin: 2010*. U.S. Census Bureau, March. www.census.gov/prod/cen2010/briefs/c2010br-02.pdf.

Hunter, James Davison. 1992. *Culture Wars: The Struggle to Control the Family, Art, Education, Law, and Politics in America*. New York: Basic Books.

Jacobs, Lawrence R., and Theda Skocpol. 2010. *Health Care Reform and American Politics.* New York: Oxford University Press.

Jacobson, Gary C. 2000. "Party Polarization in National Politics: The Electoral Connection." In Jon R. Bond and Richard Fleisher, Editors, *Polarized Politics: Congress and the President in a Partisan Era.* Washington, D.C.: Congressional Quarterly Press. 9–30.

——. 2003. "Party Polarization in Presidential Support: The Electoral Connection." *Congress and the Presidency.* Vol. 30, No. 1 (Spring): 1—36.

——. 2007. *A Divider, Not a Uniter: George W. Bush and the American People.* New York: Pearson/Longman.

James, Scott C. 2000. *Presidents, Parties, and the State: A Party System Perspective on Democratic Regulatory Choice.* New York: Cambridge University Press.

Johnson, Kirk. 2012. "G.O.P. Plays to Hispanic Fears About Economy." *New York Times.* March 16. A1.

Jones, Jeffrey M. 2010. "Americans See U.S. as Exceptional; 37% Doubt Obama Does," Gallup Poll, December 22: www.gallup.com/poll/145358/Americans-Exceptional-Doubt-Obama.aspx.

——. 2010. "Republicans, Democrats Shift on Whether Gov't is a Threat: Republicans more likely to view government as threat now, Democrats more likely in 2006," Gallup Poll, October 18: www.gallup.com/poll/143717/Republicans-Democrats-Shift-Whether-Gov-Threat.aspx.

——. 2011. "Neither Party Has Big Edge on Most Major U.S. Issues," Gallup Poll, April 29: www.gallup.com/poll/147332/Neither-Party-Big-Edge-Major-Issues.aspx.

——. 2011. "Support for Legal Gay Relations Hits New High: Sixty-four percent believe they should be legal," Gallup Poll, May 25: www.gallup.com/poll/147785/Support-Legal-Gay-Relations-Hits-New-High.aspx.

——. 2011. "Republican, Democratic Party Images Equally Negative: Approval of Republicans, Democrats in Congress at or near record lows," Gallup Poll, September 30: www.gallup.com/poll/149795/Republican-Democratic-Party-Images-Equally-Negative.aspx.

——. 2012. "Record-High 40% of Americans Identify as Independents in '11," Gallup Poll, January 9: www.gallup.com/poll/151943/Record-High-Americans-Identify-Independents.aspx

Judd, Dennis R., and Todd Swanstrom. 2011. *City Politics*, Eighth Edition. New York: Longman.

Karol, David. 2009. *Party Position Change in American Politics: Coalition Management.* New York: Cambridge University Press.

Keister, Lisa A. 2000. *Wealth in America.* New York: Cambridge University Press.

——. 2005. *Getting Rich: America's New Rich and How They Got that Way.* New York: Cambridge University Press.

Keith, Bruce E., David B. Magleby, Candice J. Nelson, Elizabeth Orr, Mark C. Westlye, and Raymond E. Wolfinger. 1992. *The Myth of the Independent Voter.* Berkeley: University of California Press, 1992.

Keyssar, Alexander. 2000. *The Right to Vote: The Contested History of Democracy in the United States.* New York: Basic Books.

King, Desmond S., and Rogers M. Smith. 2011. *Still a House Divided.* Princeton, NJ: Princeton University Press.

Klein, Joe. 2011. "Stuck in the Middle," *Time*, October 10, 2011, 25.

——. 2011. "Middle of the Road," *Time*, October 24, 2011, 30.

Klinkner, Philip A. 1993. *The Losing Parties: Out-Party National Committees, 1956–1993*. New Haven, CT: Yale University Press.

Koger, Gregory, Seth Masket, and Hans Noel. 2009. "Partisan Webs: Information Exchange and Party Networks." *British Journal of Political Science*. Vol. 39, No. 3 (July): 633–653.

——. 2010. "Cooperative Party Factions in American Politics." *American Politics Research*. Vol. 38, No. 1 (January): 33–53.

Kohut, Andrew. 2012. "Don't Mind the Gap," *New York Times,* January 26: http:// campaignstops.blogs.nytimes.com/2012/01/26/dont-mind-the-gap/?scp=1&sq= Don't%20mind%20the%20gap&st=cse.

Kolodny, Robin, and Diana Dwyre. 1998. "Party-Orchestrated Activities for Legislative Party Goals." *Party Politics*. Vol. 4, No. 3 (July): 275–295.

Kousser, Thad. 2004. *Term Limits and the Dismantling of State Legislative Professionalism*. New York: Cambridge University Press.

Kuhn, David Paul. 2007. *The Neglected Voter: White Men and the Democratic Dilemma*. New York: Palgrave Macmillan.

——. 2012. "The Partisan Industrial Complex," Real Clear Politics, www.realclear politics.com/articles/2009/09/24/the_partisan_industrial_complex__98407.html.

Ladd, Everett Carll. 1976–1977. "Liberalism Turned Upside Down: The Inversion of the New Deal Order." *Political Science Quarterly*. Vol. 91, No. 4 (Winter): 577–600.

——. 1984. "Is Election '84 Really a Class Struggle?" *Public Opinion*, (April / May): 41–51.

——. 1997. "1996 Vote: The 'No Majority' Realignment Continues." *Political Science Quarterly*. Vol. 112, No. 1 (Spring): 1–18.

Ladd, Everett Carll and Charles Hadley. 1975. *Transformations of the American Party System*. New York: W.W. Norton.

Ladd, Jonathan M. 2012. "Why Americans Hate the Media and How It Matters." Princeton, NJ: Princeton University Press.

Landler, Mark. 2011. "On Gay Rights, Obama Lets Surrogates Lead," *New York Times*, December 30: www.nytimes.com/2011/12/31/us/politics/on-gay-rights-obama-lets-surrogates-take-the-lead.html.

Langer, Gary. 2005. "Poll: Ethical Issues Tar Bush Administration," ABC News, October 30: http://abcnews.go.com/Politics/PollVault/story?id=1264205.

Layman, Geoffrey C. 1999. "'Cultural Wars' in the American Party System." *American Politics Quarterly*. Vol. 27, No. 1 (January): 89–121.

——. 2001. *The Great Divide: Religious and Cultural Conflict in American Party Politics*. New York: Columbia University Press.

——, and Thomas M. Carsey. 2002. "Party Polarization and 'Conflict Extension' in the American Electorate." *American Journal of Political Science*. Vol. 46, No. 4 (October): 786–802.

——, ——, and Julianna Menasce Horowitz. 2006. "Party Polarization in American Politics: Characteristics, Causes, and Consequences." *Annual Review of Political Science*. Vol. 9: 83–110.

——, ——, John C. Green, Richard Herrera, and Rosalyn Cooperman. 2010, "Party Polarization, Party Commitment, and Conflict Extension among American Party Activists." *American Political Science Review*, Vol. 104, No. 2 (May): 324–46.

Lessig, Lawrence. 2011. *Republic, Lost: How Money Corrupts Congress—and a Plan to Stop It,* New York: Twelve.

Levendusky, Matthew. 2009. *The Partisan Sort: How Liberals Became Democrats and Conservatives Became Republicans.* Chicago: University of Chicago Press.

Lichtblau, Eric. 2011. "Economic Downturn Took a Detour at Capitol Hill," *New York Times,* December 26. A1.

Lipset, Seymour Martin. 2007. *American Exceptionalism: A Double-Edged Sword.* New York: W.W. Norton.

Liscio, Rebekah, Jeffrey M. Stonecash, and Mark D. Brewer. 2010. "Unintended Consequences: Republican Strategy and Winning and Losing Voters." in John C. Green and Daniel J. Coffey, Editors. *The State of the Parties*, Sixth Edition. New York: Rowman & Littlefield. 255–270.

MacInnes, Gordon. 1996. *Wrong, for All the Right Reasons: How White Liberals Have Been Undone by Race.* New York: New York University Press.

Mackenzie, G. Calvin, and Robert Weisbrot. 2008. *The Liberal Hour: Washington and the Politics of Change in the 1960s.* New York: Penguin Press.

Madison, James, Alexander Hamilton, and John Jay. 1987 [originally 1788]. Federalist No. 10. *The Federalist Papers.* Edited by Isaac Kramnick. New York: Viking Penguin. 122–128.

Maisel, L. Sandy, and Mark D. Brewer. 2011. *Parties and Elections in America*, Sixth Edition. New York: Rowman & Littlefield.

Masket, Seth E. 2009. *No Middle Ground: How Informal Party Organizations Control Nominations and Polarize Legislatures.* Ann Arbor: University of Michigan Press.

Mason, Robert. 2004. *Richard Nixon and the Quest for a New Majority.* Chapel Hill: University of North Carolina Press.

Mayhew, David R. 1974. *The Electoral Connection.* New Haven, CT: Yale University Press.

———. 1974. "Congressional Elections: The Case of the Vanishing Marginals." *Polity.* Vol. 6: 295–317.

McCarty, Nolan, Keith T. Poole, and Howard Rosenthal. 2006. *Polarized America: The Dance of Ideology and Unequal Riches.* Cambridge, MA: M.I.T. Press.

McGhee, Eric. 2008. "National Tides and Local Results in US House Elections." *British Journal of Political Science.* Vol. 38, No. 4 (October): 719–783.

Mellow, Nicole. 2008. *The State of Disunion: Regional Sources of Modern American Partisanship.* Baltimore: Johns Hopkins University Press.

Menefee-Libey, David. 2000. *The Triumph of Candidate-Centered Politics.* New York: Chatham House.

Mettler, Suzanne. 2011. *The Submerged State: How Invisible Government Policies Undermine American Democracy.* Chicago: University of Chicago Press.

Migration Policy Institute. N.d.: www.migrationinformation.org/datahub/historical trends.cfm#history.

Milkis, Sidney M., and Jerome M. Mileur, Editors. 2006. *The Great Society and the High Tide of Liberalism.* Amherst: University of Massachusetts Press.

Millbank, Dana. 2012. "Roe v. Wade's Greedy Offspring." *Washington Post.* January 17: www.washingtonpost.com/opinions/roe-v-wade-and-the-dishonest-industry-it-spawned/2012/01/17/gIQAaf5T6P_story.html.

Monroe, J. P. 2001. *The Political Party Matrix: The Persistence of Organization.* Albany: State University of New York Press.

Morgan, Edmund S. 1988. *Inventing the People: The Rise of Popular Sovereignty in England and America*. New York: W. W. Norton.

Morin, Rich. 2012. "Rising Share of Americans See Conflict Between Rich and Poor," Pew Research Center, January 11: www.pewsocialtrends.org/2012/01/11/rising-share-of-americans-see-conflict-between-rich-and-poor/?src=prc-headline.

Mufson, Steve. 2012. "Voters Blame President for Gas Prices, Experts Say Not So Fast," *Washington* Post, March 13: www.washingtonpost.com/business/economy/voters-blame-president-for-gas-prices-experts-say-not-so-fast/2012/03/12/gIQA8fsO8R_story.html?wpisrc=nl_headlines.

Murray, Charles. 1994. *Losing Ground: American Social Policy, 1950–1980*, Tenth Anniversary Edition. New York: Basic Books.

———. 2012. *Coming Apart: The State of White America, 1960–2010*. New York: Crown Forum.

New York Times. 2011. Solyndra, *New York Times*, November 17: http://topics.nytimes.com/top/news/business/companies/solyndra/index.html?offset=0&s=newest.

Newport, Frank. 2005. "The Terri Schiavo Case in Review," Gallup Poll, April 1: www.gallup.com/poll/15475/Terri-Schiavo-Case-Review.aspx.

———. 2009. "Obama Gets Highest Approval on Iraq, Lowest on Deficit," Gallup Poll, September 17: www.gallup.com/poll/122981/Obama-Gets-Highest-Approval-Iraq-Lowest-Deficit.aspx.

———. 2011. Frank Newport, "Americans Blame Wasteful Government Spending for Deficit: Prefer cutting spending over raising taxes as way for Congress to reduce deficit," Gallup Poll, April 29: www.gallup.com/poll/147338/Americans-Blame-Wasteful-Government-Spending-Deficit.aspx.

———. 2011. "For First Time, Majority of Americans Favor Legal Gay Marriage: Republicans and older Americans remain opposed," Gallup Poll, May 20: www.gallup.com/poll/147662/First-Time-Majority-Americans-Favor-Legal-Gay-Marriage.aspx.

———. 2011. "Americans Again Call for Compromise in Washington," Gallup Poll, September 26: www.gallup.com/poll/149699/Americans-Again-Call-for-Compromise-Washington.aspx.

———. 2011. "Congress Ends 2011 with Record-Low 11% Approval: Annual average for 2011, 17%, also lowest in Gallup history," Gallup Poll, December 19: www.gallup.com/poll/151628/Congress-Ends-2011-Record-Low-Approval.aspx.

———. 2012. "Americans Divided on Whether U.S. Economic System Is Unfair: More than 6 in 10 say it is fair to them personally," Gallup Poll, January 25: www.gallup.com/poll/152186/Americans-Divided-Whether-Economic-System-Unfair.aspx.

Olasky, Marvin. 1992. *The Tragedy of American Compassion*. Washington, D.C.: Regnery Publishing.

Olson, Laura R. 2010. "Religion, Moralism, and the Cultural Wars: Competing Moral Visions." In Jeffrey M. Stonecash, Editor, *New Directions in American Political Parties*. New York: Routledge. 148–165.

Packer, George. 2010. "The Empty Chamber: Just how broken is the Senate?" *The New Yorker*, August 9: www.newyorker.com/reporting/2010/08/09/100809fa_fact_packer.

Page, Benjamin I. 1992. *The Rational Public: Fifty Years of Trends in Americans' Policy Preferences*. Chicago: University of Chicago Press.

———, and Lawrence R. Jacobs. 2009. *Class War? What Americans Really Think about Economic Inequality*. Chicago: University of Chicago Press.

Passel, Jeffrey, and D'Vera Cohn. 2011. "Unauthorized Immigrant Population: National and state trends, 2010," Pew Hispanic Center, February 1: www.pewhispanic.org/2011/02/01/unauthorized-immigrant-population-brnational-and-state-trends-2010/.

Patterson, Thomas E. 1993. *Out of Order*. New York: Alfred A. Knopf.

Pear, Robert. 2012. "House G.O.P. Hesitates on Birth Control Fight," *New York Times*, March 16. A16.

Perlstein, Rick. 2001. *Before the Storm*. New York: Hill and Wang.

———. 2008. *Nixonland: The Rise of a President and the Fracturing of America*. New York: Scribner.

Pew Research Center. 2009. "Partisanship and Cable News Audiences," October 30: http://pewresearch.org/pubs/1395/partisanship-fox-news-and—other-cable-news-audiences.

———. 2010. "Government Economic Policies Seen as Boon for Banks and Big Business, Not Middle Class or Poor," July 19: http://pewresearch.org/pubs/1670/large-majorities-say-govt-stimulus-policies-mostly-helped-banks-financial-institutions-not-middle-class-or-poor.

———. 2010. "Growing Number of Americans Say Obama is a Muslim," August 19: http://pewresearch.org/pubs/1701/poll-obama-muslim-christian-church-out-of-politics-political-leaders-religious.

———. 2010. "Americans Spending More Time Following the News," September 12: www.people-press.org/2010/09/12/section-1-watching-reading-and-listening-to-the-news/.

———. 2010. "Public Trust in Government, 1958–2010," www.people-press.org/2010/04/18/public-trust-in-government-1958–2010/.

———. 2011. "More Blame Wars than Domestic Spending or Tax Cuts for Nation's Debt: Jobs are top economic worry, deficit concerns rise," June 7: www.people-press.org/2011/06/07/more-blame-wars-than-domestic-spending-or-tax-cuts-for-nations-debt/.

———. 2011. "Internet Gains on Television as Public's Main News Source." January 4. www.people-press.org/2011/01/04/internet-gains-on-television-as-publics-main-news-source/2/.

———. 2011. *Wealth Gaps Rise to Record Highs Between Whites, Blacks, and Hispanics.* Washington, D.C., July 26.

———. 2011. "What the Public Knows—In Words and Pictures," November 7: www.people-press.org/2011/11/07/what-the-public-knows-in-words-and-pictures/?src=prc-headline.

———. 2012. "Cable Leads the Pack as Campaign News Source," February 7: www.people-press.org/2012/02/07/cable-leads-the-pack-as-campaign-news-source/.

Phillips, Kevin P. 1969. *The Emerging Republican Majority*. New Rochelle, NY: Arlington House.

———. 2002. *Wealth and Democracy*. New York: Broadway Books.

Plotke, David. 1996. *Building a Democratic Political Order: Reshaping American Liberalism in the 1930s and 1940s*. New York: Cambridge University Press.

Polsby, Nelson. 2004. *How Congress Evolves: Social Bases of Institutional Change*. New York: Oxford University Press.

Prior, Markus. 2007. *Post-Broadcast Democracy*. New York: Cambridge University Press, 2007.

Pugliese, Anita, and Julie Ray. 2011. "Fewer Americans, Europeans View Global Warming as a Threat Worldwide, 42% See Serious Risk, Similar to 2007–2008," Gallup Poll, April 20: www.gallup.com/poll/147203/Fewer-Americans-Europeans-View-Global-Warming-Threat.aspx.

Quinnipiac University Poll. 2011. "Voters Blame Bush Over Obama 2–1 for Financial Mess," July 14: www.quinnipiac.edu/institutes-and-centers/polling-institute/national/release-detail?ReleaseID=1624.

Rae, Nicol C. 1989. *The Decline and Fall of the Liberal Republicans from 1952 to the Present.* New York: Oxford University Press.

——. 1998. *Conservative Reformers: The Republican Freshmen and the Lessons of the 104th Congress.* Armonk, NY: M.E. Sharpe.

Reiter, Howard L., and Jeffrey M. Stonecash. 2011. *Counter-Realignment: Political Change in the Northeast.* New York: Cambridge University Press.

Remnick, David. 2011. "Obama and Gay Marriage," *The New Yorker,* June 22: www.newyorker.com/online/blogs/newsdesk/2011/06/obama-and-gay-marriage.html.

Rohde, David W. 1991. *Parties and Leaders in the Postreform House.* Chicago: University of Chicago Press.

Rohde, David, and John Aldrich. 2010. "Consequences of Electoral and Institutional Change: The Evolution of Conditional Party Government in the U.S. House of Representatives." In Jeffrey M. Stonecash, Editor, *New Directions in American Political Parties.* New York: Routledge. 234–250.

Rosenblum, Nancy L. 2008. *On the Side of the Angels: An Appreciation of Parties and Partisanship.* Princeton, NJ: Princeton University Press.

Ruthenberg, Jim, and Jeff Zeleny. 2011. "Democrats Outrun by a 2-Year G.O.P. Comeback Plan," *New York Times,* November 3. At: www.nytimes.com/2010/11/04/us/politics/04campaign.html?scp=37&sq=Republican%20political%20plan&st=cse.

Saad, Lydia. 2001. "Gallup Consumer Indicator Turns Negative for First Time Since 1993: Declining confidence may reflect partisan politics as well as economic concerns," Gallup Poll, August 30: www.gallup.com/poll/4837/Gallup-Consumer-Indicator-Turns-Negative-First-Time-Since-1993.aspx.

——. 2005. "Congress Gets Thumbs Down for Stepping Into Schiavo Case," Gallup Poll, April 7: www.gallup.com/poll/15541/Congress-Gets-Thumbs-Down-Stepping-Into-Schiavo-Case.aspx.

——. 2006. "Is Consumer Confidence More Politics Than Economics? Republicans and Democrats give vastly different ratings of nation's economy," Gallup Poll, November 2: www.gallup.com/poll/25303/Consumer-Confidence-More-Politics-Than-Economics.aspx.

——. 2011. "Americans Express Historic Negativity Toward U.S. Government," Gallup Poll, September 26: www.gallup.com/poll/149678/Americans-Express-Historic-Negativity-Toward-Government.aspx.

Sanders, Elizabeth. 1999. *Roots of Reform: Farmers, Workers, and the American State.* Chicago: University of Chicago Press.

Saulny, Susan. 2012. "Centrist Women Tell of Disenchantment with G.O.P.," *New York Times,* March 10: www.nytimes.com/2012/03/11/us/politics/centrist-women-tell-of-disenchantment-with-gop.html?_r=1&hp.

Schattschneider, E. E. 1942. *Party Government.* New York: Holt, Rinehart and Winston.

——. 1960. *The Semisovereign People: A Realist's View of Democracy in America*. New York: Holt, Rinehart and Winston.

Schlesinger, Arthur M. 2003. *The Crisis of the Old Order: 1919–1933*. New York: Mariner Books.

——. 2003. *The Coming of the New Deal, 1933–1935*. New York: Mariner Books.

Schickler, Eric, Kathryn Pearson, and Brian Feinstein. 2010. "Congressional Parties and Civil Rights Politics from 1933 to 1972." *Journal of Politics*. Vol. 72, No. 3 (July): 672–689.

Shafer, Byron E., and Richard Johnston. 2006. *The End of Southern Exceptionalism: Class, Race, and Partisan Change in the Postwar South*. Cambridge, MA: Harvard University Press.

Sides, John. Daron Shaw, Matt Grossman, and Keena Lipsitz. 2012. *Campaigns & Elections: Rules, Reality, Strategy, and Choice*. New York: W.W. Norton.

Skinner, Richard M., Seth E. Masket, and David A. Dulio. 2012. "527 Committees and the Political Party Network." *American Politics Research*. Vol. 40, No. 1 (January): 60–84.

Skocpol, Theda. 1997. *Boomerang: Health Care Reform and the Turn against Government*. New York: W.W. Norton.

Smith, Rogers M., and Desmond S. King. 2005. "Racial Orders in American Political Development." *American Political Science Review*. Vol. 99, No. 1: 75–92.

Steinhauer, Jennifer, and Helene Cooper. 2012. "Democrats see Benefits in Battling Republicans on Contraception Issue," *New York Times*, February 28. A12.

Stevenson, Richard W. 2011. "Tough Fight Ahead for White Blue Collar Votes," *New York Times*, January 14, A12.

Stonecash, Jeffrey M. 2000. *Class and Party in American Politics*. Boulder, CO.: Westview Press.

——. 2006. *Parties Matter: Realignment and the Return of Partisanship*. Boulder, CO: Lynne Rienner.

——. 2007. "The Rise of the Right: More Conservatives or More Concentrated Conservatism." In John C. Green and Daniel J. Coffey, Editors, *The State of the Parties*, Fifth Edition. Lanham, MD: Rowman and Littlefield, 317–330.

——. 2008. *Reassessing the Incumbency Effect*. New York: Cambridge University Press.

——. 2010. "Class in American Politics." In Jeffrey M. Stonecash, Editor, *New Directions in American Political Parties*. New York: Routledge. 110–125.

——. 2010. "The Electoral College and Democratic Responsiveness." In Gary Baugh, Editor, *Electoral College Reform: Challenges and Possibilities*. Burlington, VT: Ashgate.

——. 2010. "The 2010 Elections: Party Pursuits, Voter Perceptions, and the Chancy Game of Politics," *The Forum*, Vol. 8, No. 4 (December): www.degruyter.com/view/j/for.2011. 8.4/for.2011.8.4.1407/for.2011.8.4.1407.xml?format=INT.

——. 2012. "Political Science and the Study of Parties: Sorting out Interpretations of Party Response." In Mark D. Brewer and L. Sandy Maisel, Editors, *The Parties Respond*, Fifth Edition. Boulder, CO: Westview Press.

——. 2013. *Party Pursuits and the Presidential–House Election Connection, 1900–2008*. New York: Cambridge University Press.

——, Mark D. Brewer, and Mack D. Mariani. 2003. *Diverging Parties: Social Change, Realignment, and Party Polarization*. Boulder, CO: Westview Press.

Stroud, Natalie Jomini. 2008. "Media Use and Political Predispositions: Revisiting the Concept of Selective Exposure." *Political Behavior*, Vol. 30, No. 3: 341–366.

Sulkin, Tracy. 2011. *The Legislative Legacy of Congressional Campaigns.* New York: Cambridge University Press.

Sundquist, James L. 1983. *Dynamics of the Party System: Alignment and Realignment of Political Parties in the United States.* Revised Edition. Washington, D.C.: Brookings Institution.

Swing State Project. 2011. "Racial Composition Change by CD," April 12: http://swingstateproject.com/diary/8688/racial-composition-change-by-cd.

Teixeira, Ruy A., and Joel Rogers. 2000. *America's Forgotten Majority: Why the White Working Class Still Matters.* New York: Basic Books.

Theriault, Sean M. 2008. *Party Polarization in Congress.* New York: Cambridge University Press.

Tocqueville, Alexis de. 1969. *Democracy in America.* Translated by George Lawrence. Edited by J.P. Mayer. Garden City: Anchor / Doubleday Anchor, 1969.

Tufte, Edward R. 1973. "The Relationship Between Seats and Votes in Two-Party Systems." *American Political Science Review.* Vol. 67, No. 2 (June): 540–554.

Tumulty, Karen. 2012. "Recent Debate over Contraception Comes as GOP Loses Gains among Women," *Washington Post*, March 9: www.washingtonpost.com/politics/republicans-suffer-among-female-voters/2012/03/08/gIQANzfM1R_story.html.

Wald, Matthew. 2011. "House Panel Votes to Subpoena Solyndra Documents," November 3: http://green.blogs.nytimes.com/2011/11/03/house-panel-votes-to-subpoena-solyndra-documents/?ref=solyndrahttp://green.blogs.nytimes.com/2011/11/03/house-panel-votes-to-subpoena-solyndra-documents/?ref=solyndra.

Wapshott, Nicholas. 2011. *Keynes Hayek: The Clash that Defined Modern Economics.* New York: W.W. Norton.

Ware, Alan. 2006. *The Democratic Party Heads North, 1877–1962.* New York: Cambridge University Press.

Washington Post. 2012. "President Obama Faces Stiffly Divided Electorate to Start Fourth Year in Office." www.washingtonpost.com/politics/president-obama-faces-stiffly-divided-electorate-to-start-fourth-year-in-office/2012/01/17/gIQAwEkp6P_graphic.html.

———. 2012. "Gas Prices in Context," *Washington Post,* March 13: www.washingtonpost.com/wp-srv/special/opinions/gas-prices/.

Washington Post/ABC News Poll. 2003. "Bush Faces Rising Public Doubts On Credibility and Casualties Alike," *Washington Post*, July 10: http://abcnews.go.com/images/pdf/929a1BushIraq.pdf.

Wattenberg, Martin P. 1981. "The Decline of Political Partisanship in the United States: Negativity or Neutrality?" *American Political Science Review*, Vol. 75, No. 4 (December): 941–950.

———. 1990. *The Decline of American Political Parties, 1952–1988.* Cambridge, MA: Harvard University Press.

———. 1991. *The Rise of Candidate-Centered Politics.* Cambridge, MA: Harvard University Press.

———. 1998. *The Decline of American Political Parties, 1952–1996.* Cambridge, MA: Harvard University Press.

Weisman, Jonathan. 2012. "After Many Tough Choices, the Choice to Quit," *New York Times*, March 1. A1.

Whoriskey, Peter. 2011. "Growing Wealth Widens Distance between Lawmakers and Constituents," *Washington Post*, December 26: www.washingtonpost.com/business/

economy/growing-wealth-widens-distance-between-lawmakers-and-constituents/
2011/12/05/gIQAR7D6IP_story.html?wpisrc=nl_politics.

Will, George F. 1993. *Restoration: Congress, Term Limits, and the Recovery of Deliberative Democracy*. New York: Free Press.

Wilson, Jill H. 2009. "Trends in U.S. Immigration," Brookings Institution, March 24: www.brookings.edu/speeches/2009/0324_immigration_wilson.aspx.

Wilson, William Julius. 1996. *When Work Disappears: The World of the New Urban Poor*, Chicago, IL: University of Chicago Press.

Wood, Gordon S. 1969. *The Creation of the American Republic, 1776–1787*. Chapel Hill: University of North Carolina Press.

Index